£7.45

Sport and Society

ISSUES

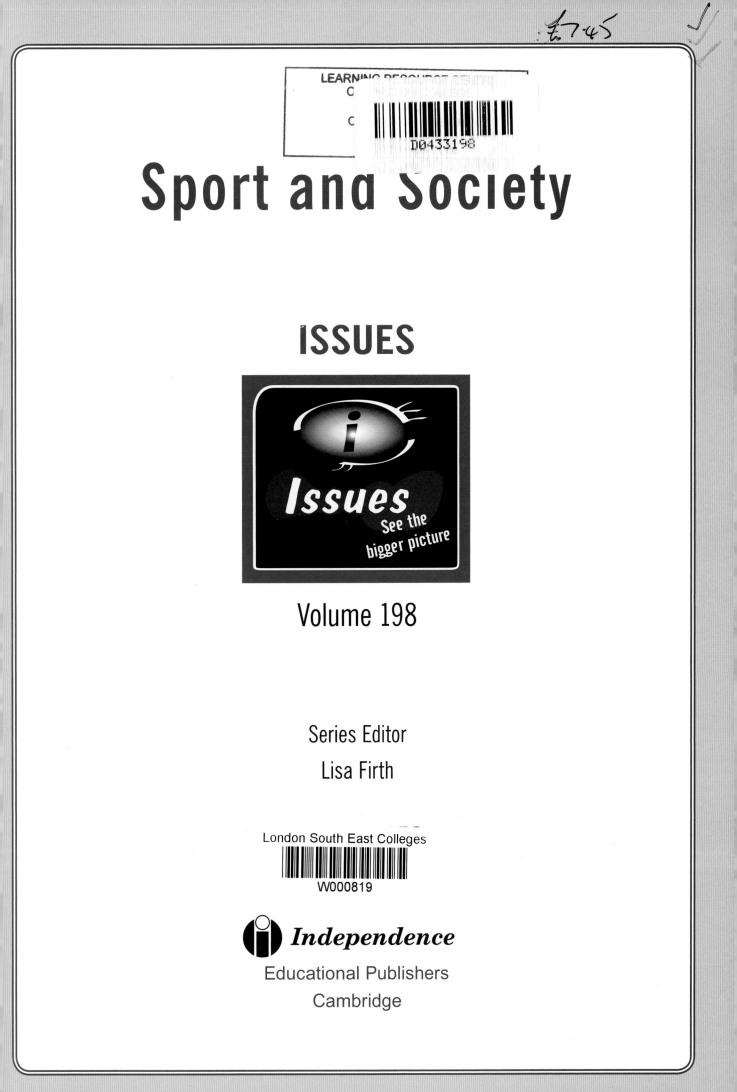

Issues
See the
bigger picture

Volume 198

Series Editor

Lisa Firth

Independence

Educational Publishers

Cambridge

First published by Independence

The Studio, High Green

Great Shelford

Cambridge CB22 5EG

England

© Independence 2010

Photocopy licence

The material in this book is protected by copyright. However, the
purchaser is free to make multiple copies of particular articles for instructional
purposes for immediate use within the purchasing institution.
Making copies of the entire book is not permitted.

British Library Cataloguing in Publication Data

Sport and society. -- (Issues ; v. 198)

1. Sports--Great Britain. 2. Doping in sports. 3. Racism

in sports. 4. Violence in sports.

I. Series II. Firth, Lisa.

306.4'83-dc22

ISBN-13: 978 1 86168 559 9

Printed in Great Britain

MWL Print Group Ltd

CONTENTS

Chapter 1 Sporting Trends

Chapter 2 Inclusion in Sport

Chapter 3 Doping

OTHER TITLES IN THE ISSUES SERIES

For more on these titles, visit: www.independence.co.uk

Food and Nutrition ISBN 978 1 86168 289 5
Energy Matters ISBN 978 1 86168 305 2
Exploited Children ISBN 978 1 86168 313 7
Stress and Anxiety ISBN 978 1 86168 314 4
Transport Trends ISBN 978 1 86168 352 6
Gambling Trends ISBN 978 1 86168 375 5
Customers and Consumerism ISBN 978 1 86168 386 1
A Genetically Modified Future? ISBN 978 1 86168 390 8
The Education Problem ISBN 978 1 86168 391 5
Vegetarian and Vegan Diets ISBN 978 1 86168 406 6
Mental Health and Wellbeing ISBN 978 1 86168 407 3
Media Issues ISBN 978 1 86168 408 0
The Cloning Debate ISBN 978 1 86168 410 3
Sustainability and Environment ISBN 978 1 86168 419 6
The Terrorism Problem ISBN 978 1 86168 420 2
Religious Beliefs ISBN 978 1 86168 421 9
A Classless Society? ISBN 978 1 86168 422 6
Migration and Population ISBN 978 1 86168 423 3
Climate Change ISBN 978 1 86168 424 0
Euthanasia and the Right to Die ISBN 978 1 86168 439 4
Sexual Orientation and Society ISBN 978 1 86168 440 0
The Gender Gap ISBN 978 1 86168 441 7
Domestic Abuse ISBN 978 1 86168 442 4
Travel and Tourism ISBN 978 1 86168 443 1
The Problem of Globalisation ISBN 978 1 86168 444 8
The Internet Revolution ISBN 978 1 86168 451 6
An Ageing Population ISBN 978 1 86168 452 3
Poverty and Exclusion ISBN 978 1 86168 453 0
Waste Issues ISBN 978 1 86168 454 7
Staying Fit ISBN 978 1 86168 455 4
Drugs in the UK ISBN 978 1 86168 456 1
The AIDS Crisis ISBN 978 1 86168 468 4
Bullying Issues ISBN 978 1 86168 469 1
Marriage and Cohabitation ISBN 978 1 86168 470 7
Our Human Rights ISBN 978 1 86168 471 4
Privacy and Surveillance ISBN 978 1 86168 472 1
The Animal Rights Debate ISBN 978 1 86168 473 8
Body Image and Self-Esteem ISBN 978 1 86168 484 4
Abortion – Rights and Ethics ISBN 978 1 86168 485 1
Racial and Ethnic Discrimination ISBN 978 1 86168 486 8
Sexual Health ISBN 978 1 86168 487 5
Selling Sex ISBN 978 1 86168 488 2
Citizenship and Participation ISBN 978 1 86168 489 9
Health Issues for Young People ISBN 978 1 86168 500 1
Crime in the UK ISBN 978 1 86168 501 8
Reproductive Ethics ISBN 978 1 86168 502 5
Tackling Child Abuse ISBN 978 1 86168 503 2

Money and Finances ISBN 978 1 86168 504 9
The Housing Issue ISBN 978 1 86168 505 6
Teenage Conceptions ISBN 978 1 86168 523 0
Work and Employment ISBN 978 1 86168 524 7
Understanding Eating Disorders ISBN 978 1 86168 525 4
Student Matters ISBN 978 1 86168 526 1
Cannabis Use ISBN 978 1 86168 527 8
Health and the State ISBN 978 1 86168 528 5
Tobacco and Health ISBN 978 1 86168 539 1
The Homeless Population ISBN 978 1 86168 540 7
Coping with Depression ISBN 978 1 86168 541 4
The Changing Family ISBN 978 1 86168 542 1
Bereavement and Grief ISBN 978 1 86168 543 8
Endangered Species ISBN 978 1 86168 544 5
Responsible Drinking ISBN 978 1 86168 555 1
Alternative Medicine ISBN 978 1 86168 560 5
Censorship Issues ISBN 978 1 86168 558 2
Living with Disability ISBN 978 1 86168 557 5
Sport and Society ISBN 978 1 86168 559 9
Self-Harming and Suicide ISBN 978 1 86168 556 8

EXPLORING THE ISSUES
Photocopiable study guides to accompany the above publications. Each four-page A4 guide provides a variety of discussion points and other activities to suit a wide range of ability levels and interests.

A note on critical evaluation

Because the information reprinted here is from a number of different sources, readers should bear in mind the origin of the text and whether the source is likely to have a particular bias when presenting information (just as they would if undertaking their own research). It is hoped that, as you read about the many aspects of the issues explored in this book, you will critically evaluate the information presented. It is important that you decide whether you are being presented with facts or opinions. Does the writer give a biased or an unbiased report? If an opinion is being expressed, do you agree with the writer?

Sport and Society offers a useful starting point for those who need convenient access to information about the many issues involved. However, it is only a starting point. Following each article is a URL to the relevant organisation's website, which you may wish to visit for further information.

Children and young people's participation in organised sport

Executive summary of an omnibus survey from the Department for Children, Schools and Families.

Background to the survey

The DCSF commissioned Ipsos MORI in early 2008 to undertake a year-long survey to measure children and young people's participation in out-of-school sporting opportunities and their total participation in sporting opportunities, both in and out of school/college. The questions were asked of 5- to 19-year-olds and the study focuses on two broad age groups: 5- to 16-year-olds in school years Reception to 11, and 16- to 19-year-olds in years 12 and above, or who are not at school.

Ipsos MORI used the LVQ (Laybourne Valentine & Partners) *Children's Omnibus* to carry out the fieldwork for the study, placing three questions on the survey every month for 12 months. Average findings are reported for the year.

DO YOU PARTICIPATE IN SPORT?

...IF IT COMES ON I SWITCH THE CHANNEL

Key findings

Organised sport outside the school day

The mean level of reported participation in organised sport outside of the school day among 5- to 19-year-olds was just over an hour and a half (97.2 minutes) the week preceding the interview with the child/young person.

Just over one in five 5- to 19-year-olds (21%) have taken part in three hours or more organised sport; 47% have done no organised sport

The key findings below are reported in terms of the proportion of children and young people who reported participating in at least three hours of organised sport outside of the school day during the week prior to the interview.

⇨ Just over one in five 5- to 19-year-olds (21%) have taken part in three hours or more organised sport; 47% have done no organised sport.

⇨ The proportion of those participating in three hours or more organised sport is the same among 5- to 16-year-olds in years Reception to 11 (21%) and among 16- to 19-year-olds in years 12 and above, or not at school (22%).

⇨ Boys are significantly more likely than girls to have participated in three or more hours (26% vs. 16%). Girls are more likely than boys to have been completely inactive (52% vs. 43%).

⇨ Those 5- to 19-year-olds in the more affluent social groups ABC1 are more likely than those in groups C2DE to have participated in three or more hours (24% compared with 18%).

IPSOS MORI

⇨ Young people aged 5 to 19 who have a disability are more likely to be inactive (60%) than those who do not (47%).

⇨ Children and young people aged 5 to 19 from a white ethnic background are more likely than those from a black ethnic background to take part in at least three hours of organised sport (21% and 17%, respectively).

⇨ Looking at Key Stages, those in Key Stage 3, 4 or 5 are more likely to participate in at least three hours than those in Key Stage 1 or Key Stage 2 (25% compared with 12% and 21%, respectively).

⇨ Of 16- to 19-year-olds, those who are currently in sixth form college (26%) or at school (23%) are significantly more likely to have done at least three hours of organised sport than those in higher education (21%), working (19%) or unemployed (12%).

Total amount of organised sport

By collecting self-reported in-school/college participation, a measure of the total time spent participating in organised sport (in and out of school/college) was derived.

Children and young people who have a disability are more likely to have done no organised sport in the last seven days

The mean level of reported participation among 5- to 19-year-olds in any organised sport in the week prior to the interview with the child/young person was just under three hours (179.8 minutes).

The key findings below report in terms of the proportion of 5- to 16-year-olds in years Reception to 11 participating in at least five hours of organised sport a week, and the proportion of 16- to 19-year-olds in years 12 and above or not at school, participating in at least three hours of organised sport a week.

For those aged 5 to 16 years old:

⇨ The mean time spent participating in organised sport overall stands at over three hours (197.5 minutes).

⇨ One in five children and young people (22%) aged 5 to 16 have participated in at least five hours of organised sport during and outside the school day in the past week. This comprises any time spent participating either during or outside the school day.

⇨ Boys are more likely to have participated in at least five hours of physical activity than girls (26% vs. 18%).

⇨ There are no significant differences by ethnic group.

⇨ Those in the more affluent social groups ABC1 are more likely to have participated in five hours of organised sport than those in groups C2DE (25% vs. 20%, respectively).

⇨ Children and young people who have a disability are more likely to have done no organised sport in the last seven days than those who do not (22% have done nothing, compared with 11% of able-bodied children).

⇨ Just under three in ten of those studying at Key Stage 3 or Key Stage 4 level have done at least five hours of sport in the past seven days (27%), but only 19% of those at Key Stage 1 and Key Stage 2 have done the same.

For those aged 16 to 19 years old:

⇨ Just over one quarter (26%) of 16- to 19-year-olds have participated in at least 3 hours of organised sport during and outside the school/college day. The mean time spent participating in organised sport overall stands at just over two hours (125.3 minutes).

⇨ Boys are more likely than girls to have participated in at least three hours of organised sport in total (34% vs. 18%, respectively).

⇨ Young people from the more affluent social grades ABC1 are more likely than those from social grade C2DE to have done three hours or more organised sport (30% compared with 21%).

⇨ Those who are in school or sixth form college (32%) are more likely than those who are unemployed (12%) to have taken part in three hours of organised sport or more in the past week. Three-quarters (75%) of those who are unemployed have been completely inactive.

⇨ There are no significant differences by ethnic group.

Composite score on participation in organised sport

A composite score was also calculated that combined the scores for 5- to 16-year-olds in years Reception to 11 participating in five hours or more of organised sport a week (in any location) and 16- to 19-year-olds in years 12 and above, or not at school, participating in three hours or more of organised sport a week (in any location). This composite score was 23%.

July 2009

⇨ The above information is an extract from the omnibus survey *Children and Young People's Participation in Organised Sport* produced by Ipsos MORI on behalf of the Department for Children, Schools and Families, and is reprinted with permission. Visit www.dcsf.gov.uk for more information or to view the full text and references.

© *Ipsos MORI 2009*

IPSOS MORI

School cricket scheme teaches pupils 'the three Fs': Fitness, Friendship and Fair play

Cricket is improving the 'social well-being' of thousands of state school pupils, according to new research.

The report by the Institute of Youth Sport (IYS) found that pupils involved in the Chance to Shine initiative displayed increased fitness levels, greater social skills and improved sportsmanlike behaviour.

There is also evidence that cricket is improving the behaviour of young people both on and off the field, particularly in deprived areas; while the so-called 'gentleman's game' is helping girls to 'overcome restrictive gender beliefs' and gain confidence in playing sport.

It may be helping to cut down truancy, too, as significantly more pupils look forward to and enjoy attending school when Chance to Shine is taking place – 53% – compared to 36% when it is not.

Chance to Shine is the Cricket Foundation's campaign to bring cricket and its educational benefits to at least two million children by 2015. The cricket charity commissioned the IYS, part of Loughborough University, to look at the impact that Chance to Shine had on the 3,000 state schools and 350,000 pupils that took part in 2009.

The research describes how the cricket sessions have contributed positively to the development of pupils' social skills, like teamwork, as one Year 5 pupil explains: 'We've all, like, bonded a bit more. We've realised that we've got to work as a team...because there's no point in just trying to be selfish and barging other people and catching the ball so you get all the pride, but if someone catches it's the whole team's pride.'

'Fair play' was a reoccurring theme in the report with pupils saying that winning is not the most important thing when playing cricket and that they just enjoy participating in cricket as it is 'fun'.

The so-called 'gentleman's game' is helping girls to 'overcome restrictive gender beliefs' and gain confidence in playing sport

Dr Ruth Jeanes, who led the research, says: 'Whilst Chance to Shine is undoubtedly having a positive impact on general cricket provision and the development of opportunities for young people, its contribution to improving the social well-being of many of its participants illustrates that it is much more than just a cricket development initiative.'

The potential of cricket for supporting young people in developing friendships and support networks was illustrated by one of the cricket coaches cited in the report. He describes how a child had been severely bullied all his life to the extent that he was 'quite psychologically damaged' and required a psychiatrist. It was only when he joined the local cricket club, through Chance to Shine, that he started to make friends and according to his consultant 'cricket had been his saviour'.

'You learn sportsmanship, you can work together and help people out,' says one Year 5 pupil; while a Year 6 female pupil interviewed says that cheating in cricket was uncommon: 'With football they (the boys) sometimes kick you and things but with cricket no one really tries to trick you and cheat. And we clap when someone does well.'

Earlier this year the charity teamed up with Marylebone Cricket Club, guardian of the Laws and Spirit of Cricket, for a nationwide drive to encourage fair play by introducing a two-hour 'MCC Spirit of Cricket' session to 3,000 state schools during the summer term.

Teachers highlighted how taking part in the programme has encouraged positive changes in pupils in the classroom. They say the cricket sessions have been effective for reducing disruptive behaviour during class and encouraging pupils to act more responsibly.

'For children with behaviour difficulties, you know they're wanting to turn themselves around,' says one teacher in the report, '...and we take them out of school and I know that I can trust their behaviour within those situations to play the cricket matches...a lot of our best players are the ones who do have some behaviour difficulties.'

The IYS report found that Chance to Shine was having an impact on pupils' fitness levels as they were continually involved and active in various activities throughout the sessions. It also improved pupils' involvement in PE and increased their motivation, especially those that tended to dislike sports, giving them 'a new lease of life' and 'an opportunity to be successful'.

The value of the cricket sessions for improving girls' confidence was notable and they were especially successful in encouraging Asian girls to become involved in cricket.

Chance to Shine has even helped some girls to gain a new-found status in school: 'It's like everyone says girls can't do cricket, they are no good at boys' sports but we are doing it and we are really good. We keep winning all the time and it has made the boys realise we can be as good as them.' (Year 6 pupil).

One 13-year-old, Caitlin Byrne from Durham, had never played cricket before Chance to Shine arrived at her school. She discovered she was a good left-arm seam bowler, developed further at South Shields Cricket Club and now plays at her age-group for Durham County.

Wasim Khan, Chief Executive of the Cricket Foundation says: 'The news that Chance to Shine is having a major impact on our schools, teachers and pupils is fantastic. We will continue to strive to give as many young people the opportunity to play and be educated through cricket.'

Ashes hero and Chance to Shine ambassador Andrew Flintoff adds: 'I think it's massively important for kids to get involved in cricket for a number of reasons. First and foremost, it's a lot of fun. But it can also teach you a lot of good things – respect, self-confidence, discipline, all things you need to grow up as a good person.'

8 September 2009

⇨ The above information is reprinted with kind permission from the Cricket Foundation's Chance to Shine campaign. Visit www.chancetoshine.org for more information on this and other related topics.

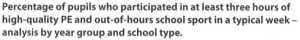

Percentage of pupils who participated in at least three hours of high-quality PE and out-of-hours school sport in a typical week – analysis by region.

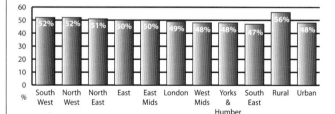

Percentage of pupils who participated in at least three hours of high-quality PE and out-of-hours school sport in a typical week – analysis by percentage of children eligible for free school meals.

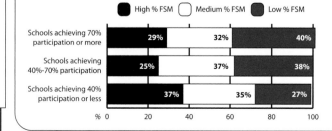

Percentage of pupils who participated in at least three hours of high-quality PE and out-of-hours school sport in a typical week – analysis by year group and school type.

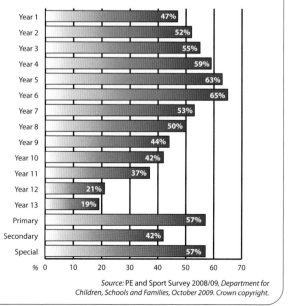

Source: PE and Sport Survey 2008/09, *Department for Children, Schools and Families, October 2009. Crown copyright.*

CHANCE TO SHINE

Olympic-style sports competition for young people launched as part of 2012 legacy

Initiative to revive competitive sport in schools.

A new Olympic and Paralympic-style sports competition for young people across England was announced today by Culture Secretary Jeremy Hunt and Education Secretary Michael Gove.

Up to £10 million of lottery funding, distributed by Sport England, will create a new sports league structure for primary and secondary schools culminating in an inaugural national final to be held in the run-up to the London Olympic and Paralympic Games in 2012.

The competition is a key part of the Government's plans for a lasting sporting legacy from hosting the London 2012 Games and to maximise the sporting opportunities available to all.

Schools will compete against each other in leagues at a local level from 2011, with winning athletes and teams qualifying for up to 60 county finals.

The most talented young athletes will then be selected for the national finals. Schools will also be encouraged to host in-house Olympic-style sports days so that children of all abilities have the opportunity to compete. There will be a Paralympic element at every level of the competition for young people with disabilities.

The ambition is for the competition to continue after 2012.

'Competitive sport – whether you win or lose – teaches young people great lessons for life'

Secretary of State for Culture, Olympics, Media and Sport Jeremy Hunt said:

'I want to give a real boost to competitive sport in schools using the power of hosting the Olympic and Paralympic Games to encourage young people – whatever age or ability – to take part in this new competition.

'Competitive sport – whether you win or lose – teaches young people great lessons for life. It encourages teamwork, dedication and striving to be the best that you can be. This will be a key part of our drive to leave a real lasting sports legacy from London's games.'

Education Secretary Michael Gove said:

'We need to revive competitive sport in our schools.

Fewer than a third of school pupils take part in regular competitive sport within schools, and fewer than one in five take part in regular competition between schools. The School Olympics give us a chance to change that for good.'

The Mayor of London Boris Johnson said:

'We have a unique opportunity with the 2012 Games to set in place a lasting legacy for sport provision and participation across the capital. In London we are driving forward our sport legacy plan that is building on the many exciting projects and partnerships already in place. Schemes such as this national Olympic-style schools competition are the perfect catalysts to get the whole country active, inspiring our young people and creating sporting stars of the future.'

Youth Sport Trust School Sport Ambassador Denise Lewis said:

'This is a fantastic opportunity to build on the excellent work that is being driven by School Sport Partnerships across the country to develop and encourage competitive sporting opportunities for young people. Competitive sport, when delivered well, can benefit young people in so many ways – from developing social skills and breaking down cultural barriers to providing a platform for self-expression and a sense of achievement. As a naturally competitive person, I'm delighted that more opportunities are being created for young people to compete in sport at school.'

Sport England chief executive Jennie Price said:

'Experiencing the thrill of sporting success is not something we all get to enjoy. But now, through this competition, more children across the country will get a taste of what it means to be part of a major sporting event. The more people London 2012 inspires, the greater the long-term impact of hosting the Games will be.'

28 June 2010

⇨ The above information is reprinted with kind permission from the Department for Culture, Media and Sport. Visit www.culture.gov.uk for more information.

DEPARTMENT FOR CULTURE, MEDIA AND SPORT

David Cameron's sport cuts will leave Britain playing catch-up for years

Free swimming for under-16s and over-60s has become a luxury we can no longer afford, according to the sports minister.

By David Conn

Four weeks of wall-to-wall football in Glorious Technicolor make the World Cup an unbeatable time to bury bad news, but that is an accusation which cannot be levelled at the new Conservative-Liberal Democrat government, which has hit the ground cutting. Every day it announces the scrapping of another planned investment because of the financial emergency it insists we are in, and sport, for all the health and social benefits the coalition acknowledges it brings, is a long way from spared.

While £9.375bn of public spending is still largely ring-fenced to build the venues and run the four weeks of London's Olympic and Paralympic Games in 2012, Sebastian Coe's pledge, always shaky, that our Olympics will inspire a new generation to take up sport, is jeopardised further by the massive ongoing cuts.

Sports facilities and schemes, often in the poorest areas, will suffer a thousand small cuts – in a nation where only around a third of people do the Department of Health's recommended daily exercise

Hugh Robertson, the sports minister, earned a reputation in his six years as Shadow Sports Secretary for diligence and genuineness in his desire to improve our nation's sporting ill-health. Yet, after just two months in office, he has already scrapped free swimming for under-16s and over-60s, cancelled an associated £25m swimming pool refurbishment programme, and committed to implementing the 25% cuts required across departments by George Osborne's Treasury.

A change to distribution of Lottery money will see £50m more come to sport annually from 2012, which Robertson hopes will compensate for the savings his department will make, but he accepts that the scale of cuts, particularly by local authorities, will undermine the provision of sports.

'This is a very difficult time and sport will take a major hit across the country,' the minister acknowledges. 'Everything is overshadowed by the state of the economy and the budget deficit we inherited. I am doing everything in my power to mitigate it, and [to] protect sport funding.'

All agree that the public finances must be reordered, in a recession caused not by Labour's supposed extravagance – spending money on schools, swimming pools and other public services – but by the banks' thunderous negligence. However, the new government has made a policy choice that the deficit must be overturned in five years and 78% must be clawed back in cuts, just 22% in increased tax.

Sport, as ever, is a perfect barometer for the effect on the nation. The top income-tax rate of 50% kicks in at earnings above £150,000; there is no higher rate for super-earners such as footballers paid as much as £10m a year, their agents, Premier League chief executives on more than £1m, or the chairman Sir Dave Richards on his £350,000.

Yet sports facilities and schemes, often in the poorest areas, will suffer a thousand small cuts – in a nation where only around a third of people do the Department of Health's recommended daily exercise – half an hour for adults, an hour for under-16s.

The 'Building Schools for the Future' programme, cancelled by the education secretary Michael Gove, earmarked an estimated 11% of its £55bn total budget, £6.05bn, for modern sports facilities to replace clapped-out old gyms. Most schools would have been required to make their new sports halls and Astroturf pitches available for community use in the evenings and at weekends. That has gone now, although Gove promises to review the needs of the 700 or so schools whose rebuilds have been scrapped.

Most public sports facilities are still maintained, subsidised and staffed by local authorities, which spent around £1bn doing so last year even though they are still not required by law to provide the option of sport.

As in the 80s, sport is certain to be a victim again, as councils must reduce their overall spending by £1.2bn this year, and by 25% by 2015. Our facilities have still not recovered from the under-investment the last time the Conservatives were in power – a 2003 report by Davis

THE GUARDIAN

Langdon Consulting found £550m required to bring the nation's 1,718 sports centres and swimming pools up to a reasonable standard, and little of that work has been done – but cuts will fall on them again.

'Sport is a discretionary service so is very vulnerable,' says Simon Henig, Durham County Council's leader and spokesman for sport and culture in the Local Government Association's Labour Group. 'These cuts are extremely worrying, that we will take a great leap backwards, and all the efforts to encourage people to be more active, which were starting to work with joined-up thinking, will go. It is being done in such haste.'

When, in June, Robertson announced the scrapping of the free swimming programme – 'not a decision that gives me any pleasure' – he said 'new research' had shown the scheme 'has not delivered value for money'. He concluded: 'With a crippling deficit to tackle, this has become a luxury we can no longer afford.'

Yet that research, an evaluation of the scheme's first year carried out by the consultant PricewaterhouseCoopers, did not say the initiative had not delivered value for money. In fact, its report said: 'In economic terms the free swimming programme has been relatively successful.'

The researchers found that across the country senior citizens and young people went swimming fully seven million more times because of the Government's subsidy – £40m from five departments – which made it free. The vast majority of those additional swims, 5.5 million, were made by under-16s, who by definition did not swim previously because of the cost.

That helped 32.9% of them do the recommended hour's exercise every day, up from 20.7%. Among the over-60s, 78.4% were doing their recommended half an hour a day, 12% up.

The Government homed in on the finding that 11 million swims were 'deadweight', taken free by people who previously paid for them, and the money spent on the scheme was not yet being repaid in long-term health.

Yet the researchers concluded that, after just one year: 'Overall the impact has been positive.' They suggested the scheme be built on to 'ensure the free swimming programme delivers the desired outcomes to an even greater degree, including enhanced value for money'. They recommended local authorities work harder to market the free entry to attract non-swimmers, and 'make facilities more attractive to lapsed swimmers through capital improvement projects'.

That gave free swimming the potential to repay, in improved health, every penny invested – and so justify the previous government's ambition that it would create one fitting legacy of the 2012 Olympics. Instead, the scheme has been scrapped, and the £25m earmarked to upgrade pools withdrawn.

Robertson maintains that despite cuts being his government's priority, he will argue to keep his budget, for the benefits sport brings.

The Lottery change will bring in extra money, and he is determined that refocusing the 2012 pledge, which he will announce shortly, will lead Sport England to try to use the Olympics more effectively to increase participation.

Jeremy Hunt, Minister for Culture, Media and Sport, has said the £9.375bn Olympic budget is 'not sacrosanct', and a £27m cut was imposed on the Olympic Delivery Authority but, in truth, the vast bulk of that budget is guaranteed.

The 2012 Olympics will be London's, and Britain's, advert to the global village, demonstrating to the mass television audience and those in the new 80,000-seat stadium, for which there is still no viable after-use, a carnival of British can-do.

The Government will not want the world to see the hangdog pools which will not now be refurbished, the schools we cannot rebuild, or that we have begun charging children from poorer families £2 apiece to go swimming once again because allowing them in for free was 'a luxury we can no longer afford'.

⇨ This article was amended on 16 July 2010. The original said Simon Henig was Durham City Council's leader. This has been corrected.

14 July 2010

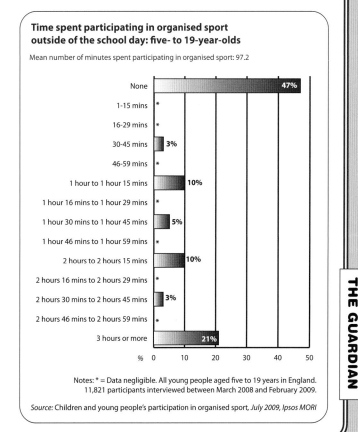

Time spent participating in organised sport outside of the school day: five- to 19-year-olds

Mean number of minutes spent participating in organised sport: 97.2

Category	%
None	47%
1-15 mins	*
16-29 mins	*
30-45 mins	3%
46-59 mins	*
1 hour to 1 hour 15 mins	10%
1 hour 16 mins to 1 hour 29 mins	*
1 hour 30 mins to 1 hour 45 mins	5%
1 hour 46 mins to 1 hour 59 mins	*
2 hours to 2 hours 15 mins	10%
2 hours 16 mins to 2 hours 29 mins	*
2 hours 30 mins to 2 hours 45 mins	3%
2 hours 46 mins to 2 hours 59 mins	*
3 hours or more	21%

Notes: * = Data negligible. All young people aged five to 19 years in England. 11,821 participants interviewed between March 2008 and February 2009.

Source: Children and young people's participation in organised sport, July 2009, Ipsos MORI

THE GUARDIAN

How to build the perfect athlete

'Talent identification' is the new buzzword in British sport – using science and psychology to find the next generation of Olympians in sports from kayaking to martial arts. How does it work – and should we be worried?

By Nick Peirce

When Rachel Cawthorn was 15, her sporting career amounted to swimming a couple of times a week at her local club in Guildford. 'It was mainly for fun,' she says, shyly. 'I tended to come in last, and I wasn't a very competitive person.' Fast forward three years, and she is, at only 18, one of the world's best sprint canoeists, and a genuine gold-medal hope for London 2012.

Cawthorn only stepped into a boat after canoeing talent scouts turned up at her school and invited the taller girls to do some physical tests in the gym – she didn't look especially athletic, but her aerobic fitness and upper body strength impressed them. Nor was her first experience of a canoe particularly promising. 'I got in one side and fell straight out the other,' she laughs.

What the scouts and Cawthorn herself soon noticed, however, was her 'feel for the water'. She turned out to be exactly the fast learner they had been looking for. 'I would never have imagined myself as an elite, Olympic sportsperson,' she says now. 'But the better I got, the more competitive I became.'

As a doctor in sports medicine, working for the English Institute of Sport (EIS) for the past seven years, I have witnessed a transformation in Britain's Olympic and Paralympic success and growth since the nadir of Atlanta 1996, when Britain came home with a single gold, and finished 36th in the medal table. In the past dozen years, the Government has allocated hundreds of millions of exchequer and lottery funding to sport through UK Sport and Sport England. My own job was born out of that money, as are the positions of nearly 400 staff working through UK Sport and the EIS to support and develop elite athletes.

This investment has had rich rewards – as demonstrated in Beijing – and the funding has fuelled a professionalism seen most vividly in cycling, sailing, rowing and canoeing, as well as winter sports such as bob skeleton. Performance directors have introduced business models to their sports and now nothing is left to chance; the 'aggregation of small gains' is constantly reviewed. Investment in quality coaches, performance analysis, scientific and medical support, technical equipment and facilities has transformed the landscape, and British success at the last two Olympics has been a resounding endorsement of the funding programme.

But however well oiled the sporting machine, it still needs athletes: new recruits to feed into the now successful models of refinement and performance. And it needs the right athletes – which is why a team of scientists turned up at Rachel Cawthorn's school back in 2005.

Traditionally, recruitment into Olympic sports in this country has been haphazard. Athletes have emerged not from a finely-honed system of selection, but from a mix of clubs, schools and families, with the right athlete finding the right coach often purely by chance. In the fringe sports, many athletes would have a sporting family; I have seen, during my own involvement in canoeing and cricket, generations of paddlers or cricketers coming through. Clearly genetics, and growing up with an 'environmental' background in sport, may maximise a child's abilities; however, it does not mean that they

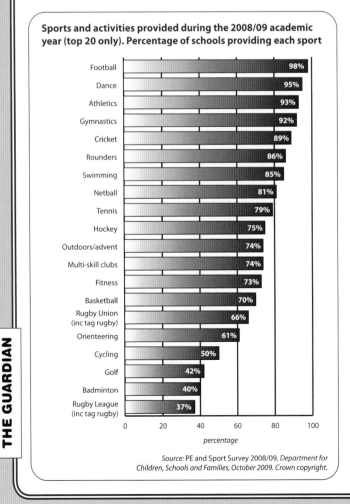

Sports and activities provided during the 2008/09 academic year (top 20 only). Percentage of schools providing each sport

Sport	Percentage
Football	98%
Dance	95%
Athletics	93%
Gymnastics	92%
Cricket	89%
Rounders	86%
Swimming	85%
Netball	81%
Tennis	79%
Hockey	75%
Outdoors/advent	74%
Multi-skill clubs	74%
Fitness	73%
Basketball	70%
Rugby Union (inc tag rugby)	66%
Orienteering	61%
Cycling	50%
Golf	42%
Badminton	40%
Rugby League (inc tag rugby)	37%

percentage

Source: PE and Sport Survey 2008/09, Department for Children, Schools and Families, October 2009. Crown copyright.

are the most talented, or that their parents are the best coaches. It remains a very limited pool of talent. Olympic teams have been dependent on the same small field from which to cultivate their talent and, not surprisingly, there have been some very barren years. Injury or illness to one key athlete could finish off an Olympic programme.

In the past decade, British sporting bodies have been studying recruiting models in other countries where the numbers of athletes is similarly limited. East Germany in the 1960s and 70s stood out as the leading proponent of what has become the increasingly precise science of talent identification. But their science served a grotesque end, creating a legacy of doping and other extreme measures that continues to blight the lives of those affected. Nevertheless, Australia has distilled elements of the East German programmes to identify the right athlete for the right sport. The pilot programmes in the 1980s, which focused on rowers, produced notable success (in the 1992 Barcelona Games, Australia won two rowing golds, their first since 1948, and followed them up with two more in Atlanta). Formal programmes introduced in the 90s led to a record haul for the country at Sydney 2000.

The idea of 'talent ID' is nothing new: even at school, PE teachers will assign the big lads to the forwards and the speed machines to the backs. Football academies snap up talent as young as possible, trawling widely and gradually discarding all but the very best. Tennis academies work on a doctrine of 'make or break them' over an average 10,000 hours of tennis practice. Some sports even use military exercises to help explore athletes' potential for leadership and teamwork. In a heavily-populated country such as the US, which is overwhelmed with athletic potential, enormous college and high-school programmes feed into professional sports, with huge 'meat market' testing days before the rounds of draft picks each year.

In the UK, the process of talent identification has had to become more imaginative and precise. Many of the Olympic sports have minimal publicity and little prospect of recruiting in large numbers (consider the number of children you know who have seriously tried their hand at watersports, or at shooting, tae kwon do or eventing). In the absence of a large pool of talent, the focus has turned to actively seeking and selecting those with the right physical and mental attributes for specific sports. And how to quantify 'the right stuff' is becoming increasingly refined.

Two years ago, UK Sport launched its first public appeal for athletes with Sporting Giants: a programme seeking talent for 'tall sports', such as rowing, handball and volleyball. It invited men over 6ft4in, and women over 5ft11in, who were already competing in a sport at county or regional level, to sign up for trials. From a database of more than 3,500, the trial system has now placed 45 athletes in Olympic development programmes, 30 of those in rowing. Victoria Thornley, who was a showjumper when she signed up, this year took gold at the World Rowing Under-23 Championships, as part of the first British women's eight to win the competition.

So how does it work? Each sport identifies its own requirements with the help of Talent ID scientists, whose background in sports science, physiology and skill acquisition enables them to research and define a profile of successful athletes in that sport – what qualities do the best rowers, windsurfers or volleyball players in the world have in common?

Many of the Olympic sports have minimal publicity and little prospect of recruiting in large numbers (consider the number of children you know who have seriously tried their hand at watersports, or at shooting, tae kwon do or eventing)

Kayaking has been an early adopter of the techniques. It established a three-phase process, beginning with a mass screening of many hundreds of applicants, measuring strength, endurance, speed and skill on special testing days. From these, 24 were selected for the second phase: skill testing specific to canoeing disciplines. Could they go from sitting in a boat and falling over to competently completing 500m time trials in a short space of time? Ten athletes were ultimately selected to undergo an intensive, three-month talent confirmation process. During this period they received full-time coaching at camps based at the National Water Sports Centre in Nottingham, including intensive conditioning, and scientific and medical screening. It wasn't only their basic athleticism that was assessed, their psycho-social makeup was considered too: did they have the right mental attributes? Sports psychologists were on hand to observe their behaviour under pressure, and to look at their sporting history.

The programme has been a startling success, with Cawthorn – identified in the first round of schools testing – one of its most notable protégées. Three years after picking up a paddle for the first time, she was competing in the Sydney Youth Olympics, where she won two silver medals. This June, she secured Britain's first ever medal in the Women's K1 500, at the European Championships in Germany, and finished fourth in the World Championships, as well as fifth in the K4 500 – the best ever British results in women's sprint canoeing.

THE GUARDIAN

But it is not all about retraining school children; kayaking and other sports are increasingly looking to recruit 'mature' (age 16+) athletes. In fact, certain sports seem to reward those who come to them later in their athletic development. Shelley Rudman took up bob skeleton after spending her teenage years training in track and field and won Britain's only medal in the 2006 Winter Games; Rebecca Romero made history by swapping her rowing boat for track cycling gold at Beijing last year; and Emma Pooley was a cross-country runner before representing Britain in road cycling. This kind of successful talent transfer was the inspiration behind last year's launch of Girls4Gold, a nationwide recruitment drive for competitive women aged 17-25 into the sports of cycling, canoeing, rowing, bob skeleton, modern pentathlon and windsurfing.

Chelsea Warr, head of athlete development at UK Sport, says that research studying the biographies of elite sporting performers has uncovered some interesting trends. 'Many successful Olympians have played a wide variety of sports, often successfully, to a relatively late age. This appears to give them a richer variety of inputs than those who have spent their entire life in one sport. Interestingly, a number of elite performers have also emerged from small cities or towns where they often had to compete against older peers. Athletes with this sporting history seem to have acquired a wide repertoire of skills, ultimately allowing them to springboard to the podium.' The 'other' sports may make more of a difference than we think – may, in fact, be a performance advantage. Another significant by-product of talent ID is the enlargement of the elite athlete pool, driving domestic competition for places and pushing established athletes even harder.

This concept of picking late-maturing athletes makes instinctive sense. Not only do they have a foundation of athletic physical development but they have had time to develop, and indeed demonstrate, stable personalities, self-motivation and independent training. We already know of a number of athletes that have played to a high level across a number of sports, including James Milner (football, cricket, long-distance running), Phil Neville (football, cricket), Darren Campbell (athletics, football) and Ian Botham (cricket, football). Once you have this foundation you can, it seems, 'bolt on' a sport's technical aspects.

Last year saw the launch of Pitch2Podium, a programme targeting previously untapped pools of sporting talent from football and rugby academies. Only a tiny percentage of football academy scholars make it into a professional career, and, in conjunction with the Football Association, UK Sport and EIS have run screening days at the Madejski Stadium in Reading for academy students, looking at sprint, jump, endurance and strength tests to determine which sport they might be suitable for. Cycling, bob skeleton, modern pentathlon and canoeing have all benefited. James Hoad, a goalkeeper at Watford FC's academy, has made a successful transition to bob skeleton, in which he is now competing on the international circuit, and hopes to represent Great Britain in the Winter Olympics 2014, if not Vancouver 2010.

However, it is not all about how high you can jump, or how fast you can sprint. In the US the major sports such as American football use a network of scouts and 'information gathering instruments' to build a picture of an individual's social background and mental profiling. Private investigators have, it is alleged, been used to check on leading draft picks. Arsène Wenger actively recruits the most talented teenagers from around the world but they will not make it beyond the Arsenal academy unless they possess sufficient emotional maturity, leadership, self-motivation and other aspects of emotional intelligence. But elsewhere the psycho-social framework for assessing the makeup of a successful athlete's personality traits is still in its infancy in this country.

What is clear is that a lot of these processes require time and investment. Certainly our understanding of what makes the precise recipe of mental and physical skills for each sport is still in its infancy, but there are several UK sports bodies innovating behind the scenes and in time we will see the fruits of these labours. For all we know, David Beckham might come back as a cyclist.

⇨ This article first appeared in the *Observer*, 20 September 2009.

THE GUARDIAN

The politics of football: should footballers be wage capped?

Information from LSIS Excellence Gateway.

Introduction

The world of professional football is always in the headlines. Premier League footballers and their wives and girlfriends ('WAGs') are a key feature of Britain's celebrity culture. The World Cup and Champions League raise vast sums of money through the sale of TV rights, image rights, replica shirts and ticket sales. On an international level, the choice of nations, by FIFA, to host the World Cup has enormous social, economic and political repercussions. In spite of the undoubted success of the sport in the era of all-seater stadia and the decrease in the levels of hooliganism witnessed in the 1970s and 1980s, there remain a number of important issues.

A Fabian Society/YouGov survey showed that people in Britain think that a fair average salary for a professional footballer would be £62,000 per year

During the 2009–10 season, the financial collapse of Portsmouth with four owners and debts of £138m highlighted the rotten state of many clubs' financial position. Outside of the top half of the Premier League many clubs are faced with escalating costs, mainly in the form of players' wages, and rising debts. The operation of the free market has allowed investors to borrow huge sums of money to buy clubs and then saddle the club with the debts. This has happened most notably to Manchester United and Liverpool. In the face of the rich and powerful owners, football supporters' trusts have tried to make their voices heard. In the 2010 General Election both Labour and Conservative manifestos referred to co-operative ownership to give fans a greater say.

The famous Bosman ruling by the European Court enabled players to leave for no transfer fee at the end of their contract and prevented countries from imposing quotas, which would have limited the numbers of foreign players in their teams. The effect was rapid wage inflation and a decline in home-grown talent in British clubs. Top footballers are now more likely to live in gated communities than in the streets where they grew up, which was often the case before the 1960s.

Football is part of society, not separate from it, and it has often highlighted underlying problems in society. In particular, the numbers of black and foreign players entering the game in recent years raised the spectre of racism. Anti-racism campaigns have been a feature of the work in all clubs, and action to counter homophobia and sectarianism has also been important. The question of civil liberties and concerns about the 'surveillance society' are also highlighted in the experience of fans attending football matches. The controversial police practice of 'kettling' (the formation of cordons of police officers to contain a crowd) was refined on football fans, and punishments meted out to fans have been criticised as infringing human rights.

£100,000 per week

The list below shows the top 20 earners in world football in 2010. Even below this very top level of football stars, Premiership players all earn between £1 million and £5 million per year. A BBC survey in 2006 also showed that age and playing position also made a difference to earnings. Strikers earned the most, then midfielders, then defenders, with goalkeepers earning the least. Championship players earned about a third of Premiership players' salaries and League One players earned a third of Championship players' wages. League Two players still earned an average of £49,000 in 2006. Highest earnings were made by players aged from 27–30.

World football top earners 2010

1 Cristiano Ronaldo (Real Madrid, £11.3 million)

2 Zlatan Ibrahimovic (Barcelona, £10.4 million)

3 Lionel Messi (Barcelona, £9.1 million)

4 Samuel Eto'o (Internazionale, £9.1 million)

5 Kaka (Real Madrid, £8.7 million)

6 Emmanuel Adebayor (Manchester City, £7.4 million)

7 Karim Benzema (Real Madrid, £7.4 million)

8 Carlos Tevez (Manchester City, £7 million)

9 John Terry (Chelsea, £6.5 million)

10 Frank Lampard (Chelsea, £6.5 million)

11 Thierry Henry (Barcelona, £6.5 million)

12 Xavi (Barcelona, £6.5 million)

13 Ronaldinho (AC Milan, £6.5 million)

14 Steven Gerrard (Liverpool, £6.5 million)

15 Daniel Alves (Barcelona, £6.1 million)

16 Michael Ballack (Chelsea, £5.6 million)

17 Raul (Real Madrid, £5.6 million)

18 Rio Ferdinand (Manchester United, £5.6 million)

19 Kolo Toure (Manchester City, £5.6 million)

20 Wayne Rooney (Manchester United, £5.2 million)

(Source: http:// thetotalfootballer.com)

A Fabian Society/YouGov survey showed that people in Britain think that a fair average salary for a professional footballer would be £62,000 per year.

Wage cap

One possible solution to the problem of players' ever-rising pay demands is to have wage caps. Some clubs are paying 85 per cent of their income out in players' wages. The result is that in the end they make losses and are effectively bankrupt. A wage-capping scheme has been successfully introduced in League Two. Here clubs must keep players' wages to 60 per cent of their income. Some people think it is a matter of time before all professional clubs introduce similar caps. A similar scheme introduced in Rugby Union saw many top players move to French clubs where they could earn more money, as there was no wage cap in France. Below are debate arguments for and against introducing a wage cap.

Arguments for wage capping

⇨ It is obscene that a man kicking a ball can earn as much in a week as a doctor dedicated to saving lives can earn in a year.

⇨ Huge salaries for players highlight the inequalities in our society and create a massive gap between players and fans.

⇨ Top clubs need help in implementing a cap in the face of growing player power.

⇨ Wage caps for clubs would prevent one or two sides buying up all the best talent. More of the money currently pouring into the pockets of a few highly-paid individuals would filter down to the grass roots of the game.

⇨ Clubs are being forced to take big risks – gambling future success against increased losses.

⇨ Some clubs spend more than 80 per cent of their income on wages and are still relegated.

⇨ Owners and managers buy players they cannot afford and put the club into serious debt.

⇨ Without wage caps more and more clubs will go bust.

One possible solution to the problem of players' ever-rising pay demands is to have wage caps. Some clubs are paying 85 per cent of their income out in players' wages. The result is that in the end they make losses and are effectively bankrupt

Arguments against wage capping

⇨ Footballers have a very short working life – 18 to 35 if they're lucky – and need to maximise their earnings for future years.

⇨ Footballers actually earn far less than some other sportsmen, such as Grand Prix drivers, boxers and baseball stars.

⇨ Top players are as much entertainers as Hollywood actors and actresses who can earn millions for just a few months of filming.

⇨ Top players earn as much for their club as their salaries, if not more, in ticket sales, merchandise sales and brand marketing.

⇨ Supply and demand. In a free-market economy, why shouldn't players demand as much as clubs are prepared to pay? If the market collapses, wages will soon decrease, as happened in snooker.

⇨ Wage caps would just complicate matters further, as clubs would seek to bend the rules using bonuses and secret offshore payments.

⇨ A percentage cap is not fair, as the clubs with the highest income would still be able to pay the highest wages.

⇨ The English game would suffer, as the best players could move to Spain or Italy to earn more money.

⇨ The above information is reprinted with kind permission from LSIS Excellence Gateway. Visit www.excellencegateway.org.uk for more information.

© LSIS Excellence Gateway

Violence down at football grounds

Arrests for violence at football grounds dropped last season, the Home Office Minister David Hanson announced today.

The number of fans arrested overall also fell last year, with no arrests at 67 per cent of all international and domestic matches.

Statistics on *Football-Related Arrests and Banning Orders, Season 2008-09*, published today, revealed there were 3,752 arrests last season – down two per cent on the year before.

They also showed violent incidents were down five per cent, with just 354 fans arrested for violence out of the total attendance figure of 37 million at football matches last year.

Policing Minister David Hanson said: 'Hooligans once blighted our national game, but we now set an example for the rest of the world in how we police football matches.

'I am pleased with the way clubs and police work together, but we must also praise fans for realising violence has no place in the modern game.

'We are not complacent and will carry on working to ensure this success story continues into the future.'

The new figures mean just 0.01 per cent of 37 million supporters attending matches in England and Wales last year were arrested. Fans were also well-behaved abroad – more than 105,000 fans travelled to 49 games in European club competitions last year, but just 30 were arrested.

The latest statistics revealed during the 2008/09 season:

⇨ 3,752 arrests were made at domestic and international matches in England and Wales;

⇨ there were 1.18 arrests per game;

⇨ the number of football banning orders on 10 November was 3,180 – representing 956 new orders imposed last year;

⇨ 92 per cent of individuals whose banning orders have expired are assessed by police as no longer posing a risk to football disorder.

23 December 2009

⇨ The above information is reprinted with kind permission from The Football League. Visit www.football-league.co.uk for more information.

© The Football League

THE FOOTBALL LEAGUE

Sports stars are no role models, say scientists

Information from the University of Manchester.

The loutish and drunken behaviour of some of our sporting heroes – routinely reported in the media – has little or no effect on the drinking habits of young people, new research has found.

Researchers at the Universities of Manchester, UK, and Western Sydney, Australia, say their findings – published in *Drug and Alcohol Review* – rubbish the idea that sports stars act as role models for those who follow sport.

'The perceived drinking habits of sports stars and its relationship to the drinking levels of young people has never been examined empirically, despite these sporting heroes often being touted as influential role models for young people,' said lead researcher Dr Kerry O'Brien, a lecturer in Manchester's School of Psychological Sciences.

'Our research shows that young people, both sporting participants and non-sporting participants, don't appear to be influenced by the drinking habits of high-profile sportspeople as depicted in the mass media.'

Dr O'Brien and his colleagues, pointing to previous research, suggest that sport and sports stars are much more likely to influence the drinking behaviour of fans when used as marketing tools by the alcohol industry, such as through sponsorship deals.

The research team asked more than 1,000 young sportspeople at elite and amateur level and non-sportspeople to report the perceived drinking behaviour of high-profile sports stars compared with their friends, and then report their own drinking behaviour using the World Health Organization's Alcohol Use Disorder Identification Test (AUDIT).

The researchers found that both sporting and non-sporting study participants believed that sports stars actually drank significantly less than themselves but that their own friends drank considerably more.

After accounting for other potential factors, sports stars' drinking was not predictive of young sportspeople's own drinking, and was actually predictive of lower levels of drinking in non-sportspeople – the more alcohol non-sportspeople perceived sports stars to drink, the less they actually drank themselves.

Young people's own drinking was instead strongly related to the overestimation of their friends' drinking and, in sportspeople only, to sport-specific cultural habits, such as the drinking with competitors after games.

Dr O'Brien added: 'Sport administrators, like the Football Association, are very quick to condemn and punish individual sports stars for acting as poor role models when they are caught displaying drunken and loutish behaviour.

'But there is much stronger evidence for a relationship between alcohol-industry sponsorship, advertising and marketing within sport and hazardous drinking among young people than there is for the influence of sports stars' drinking.

'We are not suggesting that sports stars should not be encouraged to drink responsibly but it's disingenuous to place the blame on them for setting the bad example.

'It is time that sport administrators consider their own social responsibilities when weighing up the costs and benefits of using their sports and sport stars to market alcohol on behalf of the alcohol industry.'

22 April 2010

⇨ The above information is reprinted with kind permission from University of Manchester. Visit www.manchester.ac.uk for more information.

© *University of Manchester*

UNIVERSITY OF MANCHESTER

Why do women want to be WAGs?

Despite recent scandals involving John Terry and Ashley Cole, many young women still dream of marrying a footballer and living a life of permatanned luxury. But is life as a WAG all it is cracked up to be?

By Kira Cochrane

Nicola Tappenden was a 14-year-old schoolgirl, living in Croydon, when a psychic told her she'd grow up to do something very special. She would marry a professional footballer. At the time, she had a crush on a youth team player – 'I fancied the pants off him; I think I might have snogged him once' – so she confided in her mother that she thought it might be him. It wasn't.

Then Tappenden left school, won a competition to become a Page 3 girl, and met the then West Ham United player Bobby Zamora. 'Two of my friends had stayed at his house, so they invited me over,' she says. 'He got in from football, and he was like, "Oh my God! When I left there were two Page 3 girls in my house, and now there are three!"'

Tappenden and Zamora started dating but again, the relationship didn't work out. Then she met Simon Walton, a 'journeyman' footballer who has had spells at nine different clubs in six years, in a branch of Nando's, and they went on a date. Fifteen months ago, the pair had a baby girl, Poppy, and now they're engaged. That psychic's prediction should soon come true.

Tappenden is living many young girls' dream. She's a kind, appealing woman – chatting openly about everything from her PMT to her worries about being a good mother – and I believe her completely when she says that she didn't date Zamora for the publicity. But she admits it raised her profile: she appeared on TV shows including *WAGs Boutique* and *Celebrity Big Brother*, began an online clothing business, and is now bringing out a single, *Drunk*.

And yet, when I ask if she could recommend being a footballer's girlfriend, Tappenden says no. 'The money is great for those lads... but if you could get the same amount and have a nine-to-five job, I'd say f**k the football. And I'm telling you now, if anything ever happens between me and Simon, I'll never look at another footballer... I think it's a bit of a curse on a relationship.'

Cheryl Cole and Toni Terry might well agree. The past few weeks have cast an ugly light on the lot of a footballer's wife, starting with the allegations of John Terry's affair with Vanessa Perroncel – the former partner of his England team-mate Wayne Bridge and friend of his wife, Toni. This isn't the first time Terry has apparently cheated. There have been many other allegations over the years involving a cast of glamour models.

The Terry scandal has been followed, in the past few days, by stories that naked pictures of the Chelsea and England defender Ashley Cole have been texted from Cole's phone to that of a topless model. He claims a friend of a friend was responsible for sending them, but it's not the first time he has faced allegations of sexual impropriety – specifically, a night with a hairdresser behind the back of his pop star wife, Cheryl.

In fact, footballers can seem a singularly priapic bunch, unable to walk past a glamour model without propositioning her for a threesome. And yet, in recent years, marrying a footballer has become highly aspirational for some young women. Surveys confirm it is seen as a career option by a minority; and that many girls can name more wives and girlfriends of footballers than female politicians. There is also a lighthearted group on Facebook called 'When I grow up I want to be a WAG', and an instructional book called *WAG Don't Wannabe: How to Date Footballers – and Survive!*

But the living, breathing proof is the women in bars and clubs who try to pay bouncers to point out all the players. A member of staff at Newz, a Liverpool bar that's popular with many of the city's highly-paid footballers, says that 'even when a reserve team player arrives, the girls go completely wild: they're all over him. It's ridiculous. You really have to see it to believe it.'

Of course WAGs, the acronym used to describe the wives and girlfriends of footballers, is a sexist slap in the face; an appellation that underlines their status as adjuncts to their husbands: accessories, appendages. By the 21st century, we might have expected the idea of women being defined by their male partners to have died – along with the idea of marriage as a career path. And yet, when it comes to the WAG obsession, we seem to have regressed many decades. As the feminist writer Natasha Walter says, 'There's a really worrying hierarchy in the newspapers: that to be the wife is better than to be the girlfriend, and to be the wife of the more successful footballer is better than to be the wife of the less successful footballer. It's like an 18th- or early 19th-century idea of the woman being given value by her relationship with the man, and the more successful he is, the more valuable she is.'

When it comes to pinpointing the appeal of marrying a footballer, the short answer that's always given, of course, is money. This attraction flourished in 1992 with the birth of the Premier League, when footballers' fees rose hugely.

THE GUARDIAN

And then there's the status: traditionally, the wives and girlfriends of players have been fairly anonymous, but in 2006, when the partners of the England team descended on Baden-Baden for the World Cup, the term WAG was embraced by the media with zeal; coverage of their every move was extensive, and suddenly these women were stars. Steven Gerrard's partner, Alex Curran, brought out her own perfume and a weekly newspaper column; Wayne Rooney's partner, Coleen, published her autobiography and appeared in *Vogue*.

The scene in Baden-Baden – the sunbathing, shopping, drinking and dancing on tables – looked such a laugh that Alison Kervin, a sports writer, decided to begin a series of novels based on the WAGs (the next, due out in May, is *WAGs at the World Cup*). Their stories, she thought, represented a modern fairytale. 'If you're a manicurist earning £15,000 a year, you could go into a nightclub and, in a Cinderella-style moment, meet your Prince Charming and your life would be changed for ever. You'd have more money, every day, than you'd have had in years. You'd have the castle on the hill. You'd be a style icon.'

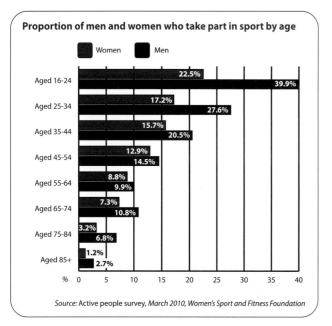

Proportion of men and women who take part in sport by age

	Women	Men
Aged 16-24	22.5%	39.9%
Aged 25-34	17.2%	27.6%
Aged 35-44	15.7%	20.5%
Aged 45-54	12.9%	14.5%
Aged 55-64	8.8%	9.9%
Aged 65-74	7.3%	10.8%
Aged 75-84	3.2%	6.8%
Aged 85+	1.2%	2.7%

Source: Active people survey, March 2010, Women's Sport and Fitness Foundation

But when Kervin began her research, a different story emerged. She spoke to a number of WAGs, and says she 'came away almost in tears, because I just felt desperately sorry for them . . . Some of those I met found it very, very difficult living in somebody else's shadow.'

One woman told Kervin that fans would open the door for her husband to walk through, then slam it in her face; that taxi drivers would take her husband's bags and leave her to struggle. 'All the normal rules of etiquette and behaviour are out of the window, because he's famous and needs to be looked after,' Kervin explains. 'She was nothing. She said she wanted to get a T-shirt printed with "Don't ask about my husband's football career without saying

'hello'" because people were always charging up to her and saying, "Where is he? What's he doing?"'

Many aspects of WAGs' lives bring to mind a sort of 1950s womanhood: they seem to be expected to come when called and, equally, to stay away when they're not wanted. (There was the notorious Manchester United Christmas party in 2007, when the WAGs were apparently told to stay at home, 100 handpicked women were brought in to party with the players, and the night ended with a rape allegation that was later dropped.)

The women face isolation and upheaval, says Kervin, as their partners move from club to club and they either follow them, and lose established friendships, or stay put, and live apart from their partners. Tappenden is well-versed in this problem – it's what she finds most stressful. Her fiancé, Walton, has moved clubs a lot recently, 'and you don't know whether you're coming or going. I couldn't keep doing it, so now we're living separate lives practically.' Tappenden is in Epsom Downs, while Walton is in Crewe, 'and I wouldn't wish that on anybody. I find it really, really difficult.'

Jadene Bircham, the wife of former QPR player Marc Bircham, concurs: 'It's a long hard slog being married to a footballer,' she says. 'They're out continuously. Their job is their life. It's lonely: a lot of weddings, christenings, birthday parties are on Saturdays, so they can't go because they're playing football... That's always their first priority.'

And alone in the house, the WAGs face the fear that another woman may be targeting their husband, that he will be the next player to jump from newspapers' back pages to the front. Nicola Smith, who dated Teddy Sheringham for eight years, says the attention the players get is extraordinary; that women 'parade in front of the boys in bars, walk up and down five or six times, looking them in the eye, even when their girlfriends are sitting next to them . . . I was actually attacked once by a girl who was doing that; she tried to hit me, but Teddy and the bouncers got between us.'

She says: 'I think football is a bit of a curse on a relationship.'

Tappenden completely trusts her current partner, but says that when Zamora's team, West Ham, went up to the Premier League because of a goal he'd scored, 'Something flicked in my brain. He was the goldenballs and I just couldn't cope with it. I thought, "Girls are going to throw themselves at him," and I became obsessed – a psycho girlfriend. He didn't give me any reason not to trust him, but when he walked out of the room I'd look at his phone, I'd try to find out information about him. I just got really insecure.'

Perhaps as a result of this paranoia, WAGs are often enormously careful about their looks. Bircham says that in the 12 years she's been with her husband, she's never seen a single 'ungroomed footballer's wife. Not one. All of them have always looked the picture of perfection.'

'They're judged constantly on their looks,' Kervin agrees. 'There are worst-dressed WAG features in the papers; there's the fact that the young girls who are so predatory around these men tend to be exceptionally pretty 16-year-olds. And I also think there are more psychological issues at play. The women I met didn't know when they were going to see their husbands, where they were going to be living next year, how much he was going to be earning. And they also knew that if he has an injury, it's all over. They're totally powerless. I got the sense that some felt the only power they had was making themselves as perfect as they could humanly be – not even humanly, in fact; they'd have various operations. If they were the image of perfection, and if the house was immaculate, then they'd done all they could do.'

There is a particular WAG aesthetic that has developed, and Kervin says she has often pondered why this is. 'The Barbie doll look – where did that come from? You'd think they'd need to assert their individuality, but they all look very similar. Orange tan. Very, very pretty. Very, very thin. And all wearing similar clothes.'

One answer seems to be that – consciously or not – the women know their role is to boost their partner's masculinity. The WAG style, with its manicured nails, high heels, huge false eyelashes and tiny dresses, is as feminised as it can possibly be – underlining these women's status as possessions, part of the package for footballers. Kervin once interviewed the England striker Peter Crouch; and in reply to the question 'If you hadn't been a footballer, what would you have been?', he answered 'a virgin'. As well as showing an attractive self-deprecation, his quip underlines the fact that girls are considered one of the rewards of being a top sportsman.

When Walter was researching her new book *Living Dolls: The Return of Sexism*, she flicked through a lads' magazine and there was 'a WAGs feature, where they had as many photographs of wives and girlfriends of footballers as they could find, either in glamour model poses – because a lot of them have done that kind of thing – or on the beach in bikinis. All the focus was on their bodies, the size of their breasts. It was like photographing a car or a house. The message was that if you're a successful sportsman, you get access to these kinds of objects. I just thought that was horrible.'

So why, in the 21st century, when women's options are supposedly as limitless and varied as they've ever been, would anyone seek power, status or wealth through marriage? The answer, Walter suspects, is that the possibilities for working-class women are still highly constrained. 'They're going into this world of glamour modelling because it's the only route they can see to wealth and success, and the WAG culture is bound up with that. No one looks at the fact that our society isn't

giving the opportunities and aspirations to young women that it does to young men, and particularly to women with fewer options and less education.'

The options are limited for working-class men too, of course, but they do at least have some credible paths to extreme wealth, if that's what they want. They can go into the money markets: a highly male-dominated industry. Or they can dream of being a footballer – at any one time there are around 4,000 professional footballers in England and Wales, although since the birth of the Premier League many more of them are from overseas.

Those that do succeed in our national game become local and potentially national icons – the 50ft banner for John Terry that appears at every Chelsea home game reads: 'JT, captain, leader, legend.' 'They're a hero,' says Walter, 'whereas the women are despised. They might get some kind of status, but they also get nasty, misogynistic press at the same time.'

The icons and images at the heart of a culture tell us an enormous amount about its values. It's interesting to note which images of women have multiplied over the last five years: an increasing sexualisation, and a media obsession with women in turmoil (Britney Spears, Amy Winehouse, Anna Nicole Smith).

The WAGs are a part of this wider culture. It's not their fault – very often, the couples are childhood sweethearts who would have stayed together had he been a plumber, a plasterer or a teacher. It is the media that has chosen to describe them as WAGs and define them by their marital status. But the idea is thus reinforced that women can never be heroes in their own right. If the obsession with WAGs represents one thing, it's surely a means of putting women firmly back in their place.

Still, at least many people do realise that being a WAG isn't all it's cracked up to be. I drop by an event in Liverpool, where women are being offered a free lip treatment, and watch as a young woman in tracksuit bottoms and false eyelashes has ten injections in her top lip, the beautician wiping away pinpricks of blood as she goes. The young woman is a cleaner who has come for the procedure with her mother. After they've both had it done, they speak to me through numb mouths, only their bottom lips moving.

'Would you like your daughter to be a WAG?' I ask, and her mother shakes her head. 'They're all cheats, aren't they,' says her daughter. 'Why would you want to go out with someone like that?'

I move on to another woman who's waiting for the injections. 'Do you know anyone who wants to be a WAG?' I ask. 'Oh no, not at all,' she says, and I smile widely. Not for long. 'All the women I know want to be like Jordan.'

16 February 2010

© *Guardian News and Media Limited 2010*

Investing in inclusive sport

Sport England today announced new investment and a fresh approach to bringing sporting opportunities to disabled people, ensuring the 2012 Paralympic Games deliver a lasting grassroots sporting legacy.

A total of £3.54 million will be available to nine national disability sports organisations, who will now focus on inclusion, integrating the sport on offer to disabled and non-disabled people.

Sport England is investing £1.54 million of Exchequer funding in the English Federation of Disability Sport (EFDS), which has announced a new strategy to increase participation and opportunities for disabled people, following a major review.

In addition, EFDS and eight other national disability sports organisations have the opportunity to bid for up to £2 million of National Lottery funding. The investment will help these bodies to develop a skilled workforce that can advise, support and guide other sports organisations as they create opportunities for participation by disabled people.

Sport England's Chief Executive, Jennie Price, said:

'With only one in 15 disabled adults playing sport regularly – and a decline in that number over the past year – there is a clear need for a change of direction. The investments we are announcing today will create the right environment for increased participation by disabled people.'

Professor David Croisdale-Appleby, the chair of EFDS, said:

'This welcome increase in funding from Sport England will enable EFDS, together with our national member organisations, to implement our new strategy to halt and then reverse the decline in sports participation amongst people with disabilities. It is an exciting development for everyone involved.'

Sport England also confirmed that a further £8 million of National Lottery funding has been ring-fenced for investment in sport for disabled people over the next two years. Sport England is working with the sector to identify specific barriers to disabled participation and how best to target the additional £8 million investment to ensure the best results for sport for disabled people.

Notes

£2 million of National Lottery investment is available for applications from EFDS and its eight member organisations:

⇨ British Amputee and Les Autre Sports Association

⇨ British Blind Sport

⇨ CP Sport

⇨ Mencap Sport

⇨ UK Deaf Sport

⇨ WheelPower

⇨ Dwarf Athletic Association

⇨ Special Olympics

No other organisation is eligible to apply in relation to this funding.

Sport England invests National Lottery and Exchequer funding in organisations and projects that will grow and sustain participation in grassroots sport and create opportunities for people to excel at their chosen sport.

Sport England is committed to creating a world-leading community sport system, and has set specific and measurable targets to achieve by 2012/13:

⇨ One million people doing more sport.

⇨ A 25% reduction in the number of 16- to 18-year-olds who drop out of at least five key sports.

⇨ Improved talent development systems in at least 25 sports.

⇨ A measurable increase in people's satisfaction with their experience of sport.

⇨ A major contribution to the delivery of the five-hour sports offer for children and young people.

18 March 2010

⇨ Information from Sport England. Visit www.sportengland.org for more.

© Sport England

SPORT ENGLAND

2012 to make history as first gender equality Games

Sport England has welcomed the IOC's recommendation that women's boxing should be part of the Olympic and Paralympic Games programme.

This means that London 2012 will make history as the first Games to have representation by men and women in every sport.

Back in December, we announced that we would be investing £4.7 million in the Amateur Boxing Association of England (ABAE) to encourage more people to take up the sport – and help talented boxers reach the top. As part of their plan, the ABAE is focusing on women and girls. Particular programmes include:

⇨ Driving up participation rates of women and girls by 10%. Initiatives include the setting up of local women's boxing development groups and providing 'summer box camps' for women and girls. The ABAE will also work with Positive Futures on activity programmes, specifically designed for 12- to 19-year-old girls.

⇨ Increasing opportunities for women and girls to box (50% of all clubs providing opportunities for women and girls). By directly supporting their clubs, officials and volunteers, the ABAE will recruit more female boxers and promote 'ready and willing' clubs focused on being more accessible to women.

⇨ Removing barriers to participation and tackling misconceptions. By engaging with the 'Make Active Attractive' campaign, the ABAE is going to create more opportunities and pathways for women boxers, providing greater female role models, training more female coaches and boosting the number of women volunteering within the sport by up to 500.

The ABAE has also recently published a guide for women and girls on how to get started in boxing.

Jennie Price, Sport England's Chief Executive, said:

'New Olympic events will bring fresh inspiration and encourage budding sportsmen and women to take up something new. Our role at Sport England is to ensure this is matched by improvements at the grassroots so that people inspired by the Olympics will be able to join, and stay part of, what will be the best community sport system in the world.'

Sue Tibballs, Chief Executive of the Women's Sport and Fitness Foundation, said:

'We are delighted that women's boxing will be at London 2012. With the sport dating back to the 1720s, it's been a long, hard fight to get to today's decision, but we hope it represents a wider move towards gender equality at the Games.'

Golf and Rugby Union (in the form of Rugby Sevens) have also been recommended for inclusion in the Olympic programme from 2016 onwards. Final decisions will be made by the IOC membership in October.

20 August 2009

⇨ The above information is reprinted with kind permission from Sport England. Visit www.sportengland.org for more information.

© *Sport England*

Sport, sex and gender

Sex, gender and the Olympics – some of the issues.

⇨ Women did not compete in the first modern Olympics of 1896. They started to compete four years later but in only two sports: tennis and golf.

⇨ Men have (to date) been excluded from participating in synchronised swimming. Historically, women have been excluded from boxing. 2012 will be the first Olympics in which women have been able to participate in this sport.

⇨ There have been a number of cases in which women athletes have been 'accused' of being men masquerading as women to gain advantage over other women competitors; there is no similar history in the Olympics of women being 'accused' of masquerading as men.

⇨ The IOC practised 'gender verification' until 1999.

⇨ The 2004 IOC Stockholm committee agreed that post-operative transsexual athletes could compete in the Olympics, but only after sufficient hormone therapy.

⇨ In 2006 there was one woman on the IOC Executive Board. There were 14 men.

© *The British Library Board: www.bl.uk*

Wheelchair sport FAQs

Information from WheelPower.

What sports are suitable for people in wheelchairs?

There are a wide range of sports that people in wheelchairs can play. These include sports such as archery, athletics (track and field), wheelchair basketball, bowls, cue sports (snooker and nine-ball pool), wheelchair rugby, wheelchair racing (road), fencing, handcycling, powerlifting, racquetball, swimming, table tennis and tennis. There are also a number of other newer sports like wheelchair badminton, and winter sports including wheelchair curling, ice sledge hockey and skiing, where people use specially-designed equipment to participate.

Nowadays there are a wide range of other activities available for recreational sport and fitness and contacts for many of these activities can be found on the WheelPower website.

Do I need a special chair to play wheelchair sport?

Although at entry level it is not essential to have a specialised sports wheelchair, many of the sports use equipment and chairs to make them easier to play and a sports wheelchair can make a big difference to your enjoyment of the sport.

The main manufacturers of sports wheelchairs include Invacare, RGK, Bromakin, Draft, Da Vinci and Quickie.

A network of dealers throughout the UK provide equipment from a range of manufacturers. These dealers include EPC Wheelchairs and Gerald Simonds Healthcare but there may be others local to you.

WheelPower provides funding for manual sports wheelchairs through our Wheel Appeal scheme and application forms and criteria are available on our website. Sports wheelchairs are very personal and are available from a number of manufacturers and suppliers. At junior level there are some organisations who do help with funding, including The Lords Taverners, Get Kids Going, Variety Club Easy Riders and Whizz-Kidz.

What are the Paralympic Games?

Held in 'parallel' with the winter and summer Olympic Games, the Paralympic Games are the 'Olympics for the Disabled'. Held in the same city and year as the Olympics, the Paralympic Games are the ultimate sporting challenge for a disabled sportsman or woman.

In 2010 the Winter Paralympic Games were held in Vancouver, Canada, from 12-21 March and in 2012 the XII Summer Paralympic Games will be held in London, UK from 29 August-9 September and will include some 5,000 athletes from around 150 countries.

How do I start playing wheelchair sport?

Depending on your age you could start at a number of WheelPower events:

⇨ Primary Sports Camps are one-day fun sports camps introducing sport to six- to 11-year-old children with disabilities.

⇨ Junior Sports Camps are one/two-day sports camps providing coaching and sport to 11- to 18-year-old children with disabilities.

⇨ National Junior Games for 11- to 18-year-olds with a combination of coaching and competition.

⇨ Sports Camps – organised by the Our Sports Associations, who are partners with WheelPower, for adults and children at all levels from introduction to elite. These camps are usually over the weekend and many take place at the Stoke Mandeville Stadium.

⇨ Sport for all – many are held annually at the Stoke Mandeville Stadium by sports associations supported by WheelPower in around six different sports. Although they are championships they also include many athletes at intermediate level and offer competition in different sports and classes.

How is wheelchair sport funded?

WheelPower is the national charity for wheelchair sport in the UK. Funded through donations and contributions from charitable trusts, groups and individuals, the charity annually tries to raise around £1 million to fund its work in providing sporting opportunities for disabled people.

Who was Ludwig Guttmann?

The late Sir Ludwig Guttmann was the founder of WheelPower and sport for the disabled. Guttmann, a German Neurologist, set up the National Spinal Injuries Centre at Stoke Mandeville Hospital in the late 1940s and introduced sport as part of the rehabilitation of his patients.

In 1948 he organised the first national competition to coincide with the London Olympic Games and in 1952 the first international events were organised at Stoke Mandeville. In 1960 the first Paralympic Games were held in Rome and the Pope called Guttmann 'the de Cubertan of the Paralysed'.

WHEELPOWER

Guttmann once said 'If I ever did one good thing in my medical career it was to introduce sport into the rehabilitation of people with disabilities.'

The work Guttmann started has now developed into a Paralympic Movement worldwide and he is acknowledged as the father of the Paralympics and sport for the disabled.

What is classification?

Sport is divided into classifications: for example, men compete separately to women; in combat sports people compete by body weight.

In disabled sport, classification is the method by which fair and equitable competition is achieved. In addition to the traditional classifications as above, there are classifications based on disability and function. The systems vary from sport to sport and more recently, classification in many sports has been based on functional ability, enabling groups to be combined, reducing the number of classifications and enhancing the competition.

At entry level, classification is usually more important in terms of 'minimum disability'; this is the term used to describe the minimum level of injury/disability that means you are eligible to participate in disabled sport.

What sport should I play?

Choosing a sport should be based on a few basic principles:

⇨ Which sport attracts me?

⇨ Which sport will I enjoy the most?

⇨ Which sport am I most suited for (physically and technically)?

⇨ Do I want to play for fun or in serious competition?

Once you have decided on a sport, give it a try. If you find it's not for you there are many others to choose from and you may find you are better suited to one sport than another. Some sports are more competitively structured and others offer more social opportunities. All are open to men and women, although some do have age restrictions for participation so it's worth checking first.

Before taking part in any activity it is always worth checking with your doctor to make sure that taking part will not cause you any harm.

Do wheelchair athletes receive much funding to help them reach elite levels in their sports?

In the UK, wheelchair athletes start by attending events supported by WheelPower.

Once an athlete has selected a sport they wish to pursue, they join one of the sports associations or clubs. Many train at the Stoke Mandeville Stadium, the national centre for wheelchair sport. WheelPower supports this training through grants and subsidies for use of facilities to the different sports associations.

As funding permits, WheelPower supports the participation of British wheelchair athletes in international competition. However, in more recent years, support for elite wheelchair athletes has formed part of the World Class Performance funding supported by UK Sport and the National Lottery.

Around how many wheelchair athletes participate in the Paralympic Games?

This varies depending on the number of sports and the number who gain the standards needed to qualify. The GB Team is co-ordinated by ParalympicsGB.

On average, how much publicity does disability sport receive in a year?

Not as much as we would like! Coverage has improved and certain publications like the *Daily Telegraph* and BBC Sport are committed to covering disability sport and the Paralympic Games. Coverage tends to be focussed around events and personalities. Channel 4 recently won the rights to cover the 2012 Paralympic Games in London.

Do you think that wheelchair athletes are treated as fairly as non-wheelchair athletes?

As awareness of wheelchair and Paralympic sport grows and facilities become more accessible, then it can be expected that people with disabilities in society will be treated more fairly. Sport is challenging and disabled sport cannot hope to compete with football, rugby and cricket, as the numbers who participate are much smaller.

It is our goal to ensure that our athletes are respected for their abilities and promoted for their achievements. WheelPower tries to ensure that there are the opportunities on offer for all who wish to take part, whether for fun or in serious competition. In order to do this WheelPower needs funding, much of which we raise through charitable donations, fundraising events and with the help of many individuals and volunteers.

⇨ The above information is reprinted with kind permission from WheelPower. Visit www.wheelpower. org.uk for more information.

© WheelPower 2010

WHEELPOWER

Talent initiative gives Britain's Paralympic potential a boost

Information from UK Sport.

By Jessica Whitehorn

To mark 1000 days to go to the 2012 Paralympic Games, on 3 December last year, the UK Talent Team (UK Sport and the EIS) in partnership with ParalympicsGB, launched Talent 2012: Paralympic Potential, a nationwide search for undiscovered potential Paralympians capable of winning medals for Great Britain at the home Games in London.

As identified via UK Sport's Mission 2012 programme, there were still opportunities to fill talent gaps within Paralympic sports in time for success in London in 2012, and so Talent 2012: Paralympic Potential aimed to support the sports to work in partnership to do so in a proactive and targeted manner.

Ambassadors from various Paralympic sports, including British Cycling's Paralympic Champion Sarah Storey and GB Rowing's World Champion David Smith, challenged members of the British public with any form of impairment to rise to the Paralympic challenge and find out whether they too might have what it takes to make the winners' podium in just over two years' time.

Over 300 individuals applied to take part in several sport-specific and multi-sport testing days that took place across the country throughout January and February 2010, and over 200 of these individuals were invited for testing in at least one sport.

The single-sport assessments have already resulted in 26 athletes being invited onto talent confirmation programmes with archery, athletics, boccia, cycling, judo, rowing and shooting.

'Talent confirmation' is an extended period of training and assessment where an athlete's progress and talent characteristics are closely monitored by coaches in partnership with the UK Talent Team, in order to make final selections for the World Class Performance Programme. This will include examination of an athlete's 'coachability', response to training stimuli and adaptation to the high-performance environment, and could last from three to 12 months. In this case the confirmation period is likely to be closer to the former, given the short timescales the athletes will be working to for 2012.

In addition to the single sport days, ParalympicsGB also hosted multi-sport assessment days where sports including fencing, powerlifting and football tested the applicants. These multi-sports days were a continuation of ParalympicsGB's successful talent programme, which will continue with a new focus on finding talented athletes for Sochi in 2014 and Rio in 2016. The sports are still making final selection decisions from these days.

Nik Diaper, Lead Talent ID Scientist for Paralympic Sport from the UK Talent Team, said: 'The athletes we have identified are exactly what this campaign was all about. We knew there were talented individuals out there, taking part or even competing in a sport already, that had no idea that they were eligible or good enough to represent Great Britain at the Paralympic Games in 2012.

'It's fantastic that so many Paralympic sports have gained new talent from this project. We now look forward to monitoring and supporting their athletes' progress while immersed in a world class training environment, in a sport they are best suited to, and, while it's a long journey ahead, we hope to see a number of them on the podium in 2012.'

'Talent confirmation' is an extended period of training and assessment

Glynn Tromans, GB Boccia's Talent Manager, said: 'The Paralympic Potential talent search enabled GB Boccia to look below the surface of the sport and engage with players who were either off the radar of the Home Countries or who had never played before. This complemented our internal search, and we have been wholly impressed with the standard of players, suggesting boccia has greater strength in depth than was first anticipated. Significant numbers of young and emerging players are set to challenge the current standards.

'From various sources, we have selected nine players onto the confirmation programme, and while we realise that these numbers will diminish as we go through the process, those that successfully emerge at the other end will form a GB Boccia Fast Track Talent Squad and have every chance of being available for selection for the 2012 Games.'

24 March 2010

⇨ The above information is reprinted with kind permission from UK Sport. Visit www.uksport.gov.uk for more information.

UK SPORT

Exercising with health problems

You don't have to forego the gym just because you have some problems with your health. As long as you take care and know your limits you can exercise with the best of them.

Asthma

As long as your asthma is well controlled, which means you're maintaining regular health check-ups, you should be able to take part in most forms of exercise. These activities are especially beneficial to people with asthma:

⇨ Yoga: Teaches proper breathing techniques.

⇨ Swimming: The damp atmosphere can be of benefit, though chlorine in the water can set off asthma symptoms in some cases.

⇨ Team sports: Especially activities that allow you to take a breather while your team-mates take over, such as hockey or football.

If you wish to go diving, parachuting or mountaineering you should consult your GP beforehand.

Exercise-induced asthma: Research indicates that about 80% of people with asthma have symptoms triggered by exercise (among other things). Symptoms include coughing, wheezing, chest tightness and difficulty in breathing. These usually begin after exercise and worsen about 15 minutes after exercise stops. If exercise aggravates your asthma, try warming up for a minimum of five minutes and taking a couple of puffs from your inhaler before you start. If symptoms continue, talk to your doctor.

Epilepsy

Having epilepsy does not mean exercise is out of bounds, just that you need a little forward planning to keep things safe. If you have regular seizures you should avoid sports which could leave you in a sticky situation should you have an attack. Generally, this means daredevil stuff such as scuba diving, parachuting, mountaineering, gliding, hang gliding, aviation, motor racing, boxing and karate. Supervision may also be needed when doing any water-based sport (e.g. water-skiing, swimming) because of the risk of drowning if you have a seizure. The Epilepsy Action website has some very useful advice on exercising with epilepsy.

Reduced mobility

Always consult your doctor or physiotherapist before trying a new sport/fitness regime. Instructors may not be trained to deal with disability, or your specific situation, so be sure to establish this before you take things further.

Gyms: Look around for a gym that suits you. Some may be more accessible than others or better suited to certain disabilities. A good gym will give you a full assessment and provide you with a detailed training programme tailored to your needs. Try to go at quieter times if you're likely to need help from staff.

More information

English Federation of Disability Sport

www.efds.net

Disability Sport England

www.disabilitysport.org.uk

You're Able – Information, products and services for disabled people

www.youreable.com

⇨ The above information is reprinted with kind permission from TheSite.org. Visit www.thesite.org for more information.

© TheSite.org

Trends for top 15 female participation sports:
Active People Survey 2008-09

Sport	Percentage
Swimming	9.58%
Athletics	3.24%
Cycling	2.34%
Equestrian	1.39%
Tennis	1.07%
Badminton	1.04%
Football	0.73%
Bowls	0.65%
Golf	0.65%
Netball	0.61%
Dance exercise	0.38%
Hockey	0.22%
Basketball	0.19%
Squash/racquetball	0.18%
Skiing/snowboarding	0.18%

percentage

Source: Active People Survey, *March 2010, Women's Sport and Fitness Foundation*

THESITE.ORG

Asians in football

Information from Kick It Out.

Hundreds of thousands of young Asians are playing and watching the game around the country every weekend.

But there is a massive under-representation of the Asian community in the professional game.

The facts speak for themselves.

There are only seven British Asian players in professional football and a Commission for Racial Equality (CRE) survey into professional football in 2004 revealed that in total there were only ten Asian players at Premier League club academies.

Within the Asian community there continues to be a feeling that Asian players have been marginalised by the game for far too long.

Popular myths

Popular myths such as Asians are only interested in cricket and hockey, that Asians aren't strong enough to play the game professionally and that cultural differences will prevent Asian players' footballing development are just a few of the common falsehoods that have hampered Asian players' break through.

In response, a number of groups have organised themselves to ensure they are providing young talented players from the Asian community with the chance to improve and progress.

Teams such as London APSA and Sporting Bengal became the first Asian clubs to play in the FA Cup in 2005. Albion Sports Club from Bradford, perhaps Britain's most successful local Asian Football Club, have reached the nationwide FA Sunday Cup Final twice, and the London Asian Football League continues to grow, attracting teams from all backgrounds. These are just a few examples of how Asians are climbing the football ladder.

Trailblazers

While frustrations remain, the love for the game drives on talented young Asians in striving to achieve the goal of joining trailblazers Rehman, Chopra, Singh and Ahmed in the professional game.

Under-representation in other areas of the game is also beginning to be challenged with the successes of Football League referees, Jarnail Singh and Mo Matadar.

The game recognised the need to ensure that the Asian community is no longer excluded following the launch of the *Asians Can Play Football* report in 2005.

Football family commitment

Simon Johnson, the Football Association's Director of Corporate Affairs, said on behalf of the football family: 'We want to create more and better coaches from the Asian communities. We want to create clear pathways for the most talented to progress. We want to ensure that, when the clubs are scouting for players, they are doing so in such a way that they can find the very best talent from the Asian communities.

'Each of the bodies has a role to play in making all this happen. We know that, and we are taking the necessary action. We also want to see the active fan base at our clubs adapt to reflect the diversity of the communities in which they play.'

⇨ The above information is reprinted with kind permission from Kick It Out. Visit www.kickitout.org for more information.

© Kick It Out 2010

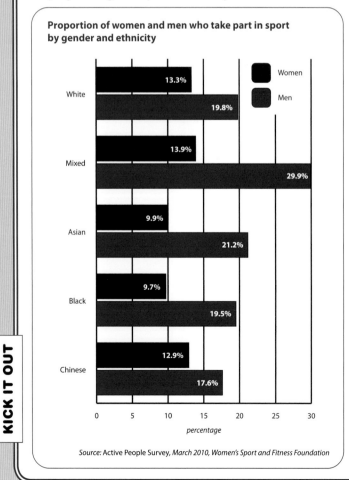

Proportion of women and men who take part in sport by gender and ethnicity

- White — Women 13.3%, Men 19.8%
- Mixed — Women 13.9%, Men 29.9%
- Asian — Women 9.9%, Men 21.2%
- Black — Women 9.7%, Men 19.5%
- Chinese — Women 12.9%, Men 17.6%

percentage

Source: Active People Survey, March 2010, Women's Sport and Fitness Foundation

KICK IT OUT

Homophobia in football

Information from Kick It Out.

Homophobia is defined as an irrational fear or intolerance of homosexuality, or behaviour that is perceived to uphold and support traditional gender role expectations.

In sport, homophobia is expressed in ways ranging from telling jokes directed against homosexual activity, through harassment to physical violence against homosexual sportspeople.

There are several other organisations and campaign groups working tirelessly to ensure that homophobia does not remain a malignant presence within football, and sport in general.

Stonewall has been leading the way in the field of gay rights for over 20 years, since its inception in 1989, and is renowned for its lobbying and campaigning on crucial issues, including the age of consent and the ban on lesbians and gays in the military.

Report

In 2009, the charity published a report calling for football to take more decisive action on homophobic abuse in the sport, which can be read in full on the Stonewall website.

In 1998, Justin Fashanu, still the only English professional footballer to come out as being gay, committed suicide. Ten years later, the Justin Campaign was formed to raise awareness of Justin's life and the continuing issue of homophobia in football.

The Gay Football Supporters' Network, which was formed in 1989, aims to promote the support and participation of gay men and women in football, and act as a medium for LGBT football supporters to get together.

In the past, certain players have been singled out by opposing fans as targets of homophobic abuse. One such player, Graeme Le Saux, spoke about the impact the abuse had on his playing career in his autobiography.

'Because I had different interests, because I didn't feel comfortable in the laddish drinking culture that was prevalent in English football in the late 1980s, it was generally assumed by my team-mates that there was something wrong with me. It followed, naturally, that I must be gay.

'Football's last taboo'

'For 14 years I had to listen to that suggestion repeated in vivid and forthright terms from thousands of voices in the stands. It was a lie. I am not gay and never have been, yet I became a victim of English football's last taboo.

'The homophobic taunting and bullying left me close to walking away from football. I went through times that were like depression. I did not know where I was going.

'I would get up in the morning and would not feel good and by the time I got into training I would be so nervous that I felt sick. I dreaded going in. I was like a bullied kid on his way to school to face his tormentors.'

Experiences such as Le Saux's are another crucial reason why the issue of homophobia can no longer be allowed to go unaddressed.

⇨ The above information is reprinted with kind permission from Kick It Out. Visit www.kickitout.org for more information.

© Kick It Out

KICK IT OUT

Leagues behind: football's failure to tackle anti-gay abuse

Information from Stonewall.

Introduction

Football is Britain's national game. Yet in 2009 not one gay professional footballer in Britain, of which there are undoubtedly many, feels that football is an industry in which it is safe to be openly gay. Neither does the game give lesbian, gay and bisexual football fans and players the respect and protection they deserve.

This pioneering research by Stonewall, including a YouGov survey of 2,005 football fans and interviews with football insiders, shows clearly that anti-gay abuse is all too common on both terraces and pitches and that this abuse almost always goes unchallenged. Fans believe that it is this abuse, from fans, players and team-mates, that deters gay people from playing football and creates a culture of fear where gay players feel it is unsafe to come out. The research also demonstrates that many others – including women supporters and those with families – are deterred from attending games by the presence of anti-gay abuse.

Fans are clear that it is the lack of any visible action by the Football Association, football clubs and their partners in tackling anti-gay abuse which has allowed it to fester on the terraces and in changing rooms across Britain. Football fans are also adamant that they want this to change and believe that football would be a far better sport if anti-gay abuse was eradicated.

Football has had demonstrable success in challenging other problems, from racism to hooliganism. The same high-profile commitment and imagination urgently needs to be applied to tackling anti-gay abuse too. This research provides the Football Association, football clubs and their partners with a clear challenge from fans. If they fail to rise to it, football risks deterring a new generation of talent and losing its right to claim to be Britain's national game for the 21st century.

Summary and key findings

Many football fans and individuals working within the football industry believe that the sport is anti-gay and the majority of fans attending matches have heard homophobic abuse on the terraces. Three in four fans think there are gay players currently in the Premier League or Championship and seven in ten think there are gay players in Leagues One or Two. Two-thirds of fans would feel comfortable if a player on their team came out but only one in eight think there is a gay player on their team. Seven in ten fans who have attended a match in the last five years have heard anti-gay language and abuse on the terraces. Three in five fans believe anti-gay abuse from fans dissuades gay professional players from coming out, one in four believe anti-gay abuse from team-mates contributes to there currently being no openly gay players. Over half of football fans think the Football Association, the Premier League and the Football League are not doing enough to tackle anti-gay abuse, only three in ten believe they are doing enough already. Half of football fans think football clubs themselves are not doing enough to tackle anti-gay abuse, only a third believe they are doing enough already.

'I think there's still an awful lot to do before anyone's going to come out at the top end of the game, an awful lot.' (Football industry executive)

More than one in four football fans think professional football is 'anti-gay' and only one in three fans think football is less anti-gay than 20 years ago. Fans and individuals working within the football industry are clear that they want football clubs, the Football Association and their partners to demonstrate leadership and make football a better sport by tackling anti-gay abuse. Many feel, however, that to date not enough has been done to tackle anti-gay abuse. Almost two-thirds of fans believe football would be a better sport if anti-gay abuse and discrimination was eradicated. Only one in six fans say their club is doing work to tackle anti-gay abuse. Five out of six fans support the police's decision to charge fans with chanting anti-gay and racist abuse at Sol Campbell at the Tottenham Hotspur v Portsmouth game on 28 September 2008. The benefits of tackling anti-gay abuse for football clubs and football as a whole are clear. Fans would be more likely to attend matches, purchase merchandise and participate in amateur football if anti-gay abuse was tackled. Two in five lesbian, gay and bisexual fans would be more likely to buy merchandise or tickets if football was more gay-friendly. One in six of all fans would be more likely to attend football matches if anti-gay abuse was tackled.

'Nothing is done to stop homophobic chants. It must be the only profession where the workers feel unable to come out and be accepted for playing football, not what they are.' (Simon, Ipswich Town supporter)

⇨ The above information is an extract from Stonewall's report *Leagues Behind: Football's failure to tackle anti-gay abuse*, and is reprinted with permission. Visit www.stonewall.org.uk for more information.

STONEWALL

Types of drug testing in sport

Information from teachpe.com

Drug testing has become an increasingly large part of both professional and amateur sports. An athlete can be called for drug testing at any time, in or out of competition. During competition, some sports only carry out drug testing on the winning team or top three competitors. Others will test by random selection from all competitors.

Urine testing

When called for a drugs test, the athlete is entitled to have a representative (such as their coach or team doctor) present to verify that the testing occurred in accordance with guidelines. A sample is provided (in view of an official of the same gender), split into two bottles and sealed by the athlete. A code number will be attached to the bottle and recorded on the relevant paperwork to ensure the correct result is given to the athlete whilst retaining their anonymity.

Following the sampling procedure, the athlete must complete a medical declaration which states all medicines, drugs and substances taken over the last week. It is important that the athlete records everything, from over-the-counter medicines to supplements and prescribed drugs. If any of these substances are on the prohibited list the athlete must hold a Therapeutic Use Exemption (TUE). The competitor, representative and official all check the form before the official and athlete sign it and both parties are given a copy.

The samples are then sent to a registered laboratory (if there is not one on site), where sample A is tested using gas chromatography (which uses separation techniques to divide the contents of the sample) and mass spectrometry (which provides the exact molecular specification of the compounds). If a positive result is found with sample A, the athlete is notified before sample B is also tested. The athlete or their representative is entitled to be present at the unsealing and testing of the second sample. If this too is positive, the relevant sporting organisations are notified, whose responsibility it is to decide what penalties or bans are to be imposed.

Blood testing

Blood testing is used in the detection of drugs such as EPO and artificial oxygen carriers by testing the haematocrit or blood count. Over time a 'blood profile' of an athlete can be built up to help determine average readings for each individual. This can help with blood doping tests in the future. The same anonymity and representative procedures apply as for urine sampling.

Again the athlete is asked to select and check the testing and collection equipment before a phlebotomist (an individual trained to draw blood) collects two samples of blood directly into bottles A and B. The bottles stay in the possession of the athlete (who is always accompanied by an official) until they are sealed in the sample collection kit. Samples are sent to a lab for testing. The same procedure applies as in urine testing, where if the A sample is positive, the B sample is then tested. Another positive result means the appropriate governing bodies are notified.

⇨ The above information is reprinted with kind permission from teachpe.com

© teachpe.com

What's the result?

Judging by the way the sample is bouncing about I'd say positive.

TEACHPE.COM

Drugs and sport

Information from Patient UK.

There are three reasons why athletes and sports-people may take drugs:

1 As medication for disease: they are as entitled to treatment for a medical condition as anyone else but both the competitor and the doctor must be aware of the rules about banned substances. Failure to heed them can have serious consequences. An athlete could receive either a temporary or permanent ban from competing in that sport. If the doctor is at fault, there is potential for litigation irrespective of whether the individual is an amateur or professional competitor.

2 To enhance performance: in doing so this could give an unfair advantage. The GMC's stance on this is unequivocal:

GMC guidance

Doctors who prescribe or collude in the provision of drugs or treatment with the intention of improperly enhancing an individual's performance in sport would be contravening the GMC's guidance, and such actions would usually raise a question of a doctor's continued registration. This does not preclude the provision of any care or treatment where the doctor's intention is to protect or improve the patient's health.

3 As recreational drugs: e.g. cannabis is a banned substance even though it is not considered a performance-enhancing drug. The authorities say that it is necessary to take such steps as athletes and sportspeople are role models for young people and hence should not take illicit drugs. However, they do not suggest how young people would know that their heroes take drugs if they were not tested and positive results made public.

Drug testing

⇨ All elite athletes competing at international level and professional sportspeople are likely to be routinely tested. However, testing may go down to much lower levels and include young competitors. Sometimes testing may be anticipated. It is common practice to test all who have won medals in major events but random drug testing can also take place. Elite athletes may also be visited by representatives from their governing body for out-of-season testing.

⇨ Some drugs are permissible when not competing but not during competition. Others, such as anabolic steroids, are banned at all times.

⇨ Some drugs are banned in some sports but not others. Banned substances can include alcohol and caffeine above a certain level. Beta-blockers would impair performance of an endurance athlete but suppression of tremor gives unfair advantage in shooting events. It may be possible to get guidance from the sport's website.

⇨ Drug testing does not apply simply to sports such as athletics and football but may include snooker, bridge and chess played at the highest levels.

Therapeutic Use Exemption (TUE)

If a doctor believes that there is a good reason why his patient needs a banned substance, it is possible to issue a Therapeutic Use Exemption (TUE) certificate. An example of one to be used for football is found at the FIFA website (www.fifa.com). They may be temporary for a single spell of illness or of longer duration. They must be issued in good faith, stating that alternative medication is inappropriate. For example, if a snooker player has hypertension, does he really need a beta-blocker?

Potential pitfalls

The problems faced by a doctor may be for relatively minor treatments such as decongestants, analgesics and medication for asthma. As mentioned above, some drugs are permissible in some sports and not others. Some are permissible out of competition but not whilst competing.

Doctors need to be aware of the possibility that patients may use an element of deceit to acquire prescriptions for substances that they know they should not have.

Analgesics

⇨ Athletes often suffer injuries and analgesics may be appropriate. Non-steroidal anti-inflammatory drugs (NSAIDs) are the group of choice and are always permissible, as is paracetamol.

⇨ Opiate-related analgesics are more problematic. Codeine is not on the World Anti-Doping Agency (WADA) list of banned substances and combinations such as co-codamol appear acceptable. It is the stronger narcotic agents that are banned. However, screening does not always differentiate adequately between the various narcotic or codeine-related compounds and they are best avoided.

Sometimes an athlete will ask the doctor to give an injection into an injured part to permit competition. Pain is an important warning that something is wrong and if a significant injury is pain-free this is a potentially dangerous situation. Steroid injections may also weaken ligaments and should not be given into tendons or ligaments.

The problem of stimulants in sport reached public attention in 1960 when the Danish cyclist Knut Jenson died in the Rome Olympics and it transpired that he had been taking amphetamines

Diuretics

The main reason for wishing to use diuretics is to produce more dilute urine so that illicit substances are not detected. For this reason they are banned. They may also be used in sports with weight categories such as judo and weight lifting. The competitor can dehydrate, make the weight at the weigh-in and then rehydrate before the competition, as even mild dehydration can ebb fitness significantly. Jockeys have used diuretics for many years. Masking substances to hide the use of illicit drugs include probenecid and this is also banned.

Stimulants

⇨ The problem of stimulants in sport reached public attention in 1960 when the Danish cyclist Knut Jenson died in the Rome Olympics and it transpired that he had been taking amphetamines.

⇨ The problem for doctors is not usually with amphetamines, as these now have few indications, but with decongestants that may be requested or bought over the counter to clear the airways of an athlete with a cold.

⇨ Substances containing phenylephedrine and pseudoephedrine should be avoided. Ephedrine is prohibited when its concentration in urine is >10 micrograms per millilitre. This probably means that 0.5% ephedrine nose drops are safe.

⇨ Saline nose drops are certainly safe and allowed but less effective. If a pharmacological agent is required, an anticholinergic such as ipratropium spray may be used.

⇨ Beta-2 agonists are banned substances but they may be used if delivered by inhaler to a patient with asthma and a TUE is issued.

⇨ Corticosteroids are also banned but if anyone needs them, whether they are otherwise fit to compete at top level needs to be questioned. A TUE may be issued. Topical steroids are permitted.

Enhancement of oxygen transfer

For endurance events, a high haematocrit enhances performance. There are three ways to achieve this:

⇨ Training at altitude in a low pressure of oxygen stimulates endogenous erythropoietin.

⇨ Recombinant erythropoietin is effective, especially if combined with supplementary iron.

⇨ Blood doping means removal of a unit of blood, perhaps four to six weeks before competition. The body replaces the lost blood and shortly before competition the blood is transfused.

Of these three techniques, only altitude training is legal. There is no satisfactory way of detecting blood doping by autologous transfusion. Techniques are being developed to detect recombinant erythropoietin and may already be used. Substances to enhance oxygen uptake and haemoglobin substitutes are also banned.

Anabolic steroids

⇨ Anabolic steroids are a generic term for male hormones. The idea behind their abuse in sport is that they promote muscle growth and protein synthesis. However, abuse also has side effects such as cardiomyopathy, atherosclerosis, hypercoagulopathy, hepatic dysfunction and psychiatric and behavioural disturbances. They may be used for hypogonadism or diseases such as aplastic anaemia but such people are unlikely to compete at an elite level.

⇨ In the 1970s athletes would take synthetic androgens such as nandrolone and these are easy to detect without any controversy. A much more difficult problem is when an endogenous substance such as testosterone is taken. The ratio of testosterone to dihydroepiandrosterone (DHEA) is usually about 1:1 or 2:1. A similar ratio is expected in women. If it is over 4:1 then exogenous testosterone is likely. Some men appear to have naturally high ratios but a radiocarbon test can detect synthetic testosterone. New ways are being developed to detect metabolites of androstenedione, testosterone and dihydrotestosterone abuse.

⇨ Female hormones also have anabolic effects, although not as marked as male hormones. Athletes who return to training after pregnancy often find that they are stronger than they were before. Oral contraceptives are permitted substances and may well be desirable. They tend to reduce menstrual loss and hence any tendency to iron deficiency. As well as making menstruation more tolerable, they can be used to adjust its timing so that the competitor is not pre-menstrual or menstruating during an important event. Their value as a contraceptive is also appreciated.

⇨ Other banned substances include tibolone, which has some anabolic effects, and anti-oestrogens including the SERMs and aromatase inhibitors. If there are genuine reasons to prescribe such drugs, a TUE can be issued.

New trends in hormone abuse

The chemicals that we tend to think of as anabolic (the male hormones described above) are not the only ones with anabolic properties and hence other hormones may also be abused. In 1989 the Medical Commission of the International Olympic Committee (IOC) introduced the new doping class of peptide hormones and analogues. This includes:

⇨ Human chorionic gonadotrophin (hCG) and related compounds;

⇨ Corticotrophins, including adrenocorticotrophic hormone (ACTH);

⇨ Human growth hormone (hGH), Insulin-like Growth Factors and Mechano Growth Factors;

⇨ All of the releasing factors of these listed hormones;

⇨ Erythropoietin (Epo);

⇨ Insulins.

Both hCG and luteinising hormone (LH) may also be used to enhance the endogenous production of testosterone by artificial means and are prohibited in males.

In the past 20 years, growth hormone (GH) has been considered as a performance-enhancing drug in the world of sport. A blood test for hGH was first introduced at the 2004 Summer Olympic Games in Athens, Greece. Further tests are being developed to enhance the detection window for hGH abuse.

Because resting or random measurements of plasma GH concentrations *per se* are meaningless, new methods have been devised to evaluate plasma levels of GH-sensitive substances that are more stable, and hence detectable, than the hormone itself.

Growth hormone and insulin seem to work together to control blood glucose but the role of insulin is much more profound than just glucose homeostasis. Insulin may be used to counter the hyperglycaemic effects of GH but it is also abused by body builders and there are reports of severe hypoglycaemia as a result. The legal classification of insulin has been changed from P (for sale in pharmacies) to PoM (prescription only medicine).

Gene doping

In the future, this could potentially become a new possibility for abuse as a performance enhancer in sport. WADA describes gene doping as 'the non-therapeutic use of cells, genes, genetic elements, or of the modulation of gene expression, having the capacity to improve athletic performance'. The potential for gene doping would be to inject 'normal' genes into the body to increase the functioning of a 'normal' cell. For example, genes producing insulin growth factor 1 to help muscles grow and repair.

Denying the charges

Sometimes when an athlete is found to have taken a banned substance, he or she admits to the fault but very often they deny ever knowingly having taken a banned substance. Cynics are unsurprised but often the athletes seem very genuine.

Elite athletes are not 'normal' people and so reference ranges for physiological substances need to be determined on their peers. A cyclist who may be burning 9,000 calories a day during competition is not a normal subject. Sprinters tend to be very muscular and have a low body fat content. Fat is important in the metabolism of steroid hormones. The people who set such standards are sufficiently well versed in sports medicine and exercise physiology that they set their standards by the norm for the group that they examine. Nevertheless, if they say that their reference range will include 99% of all those active athletes who are not taking banned substances, then one in 100 will fall outside that range.

Most top athletes use dietary supplements and the contents of these may not be as vigorously controlled as may be hoped. Contaminants that have been identified include a variety of anabolic androgenic steroids including testosterone and nandrolone as well as the pro-hormones of these compounds, ephedrine and caffeine. This contamination may be the result of poor manufacturing practice, but there is some evidence of deliberate adulteration of products. The principle of strict liability that applies in sport means that innocent ingestion of prohibited substances is not an acceptable excuse, and athletes testing positive are liable to penalties. Although it is undoubtedly the case that some athletes are guilty of deliberate cheating, some positive tests are likely to be the result of inadvertent ingestion of prohibited substances present in otherwise innocuous dietary supplements.

The beneficial effects of creatine have been shown in a number of studies. It is thought to offer potential gains in body mass and muscle strength. Creatine, ginseng and a number of other substances raise the question of when does a dietary supplement become a drug? Some people like to use herbal products in the belief that they are beneficial but not pharmacological. Some may even have been contaminated with pharmaceutical products, as with the contamination of Chinese treatments for eczema with corticosteroids.

Ethical considerations

The position of the GMC with regard to a doctor aiding and abetting drug abuse in sport is clear. However, a doctor may be faced by a patient who admits to using anabolic steroids. He does not enter competitions and so is not tested. He wants the doctor to monitor his liver function as an early warning of any damage. What is the position? He will continue to take the steroids whether the doctor cooperates or not. Would it be reasonable to warn him of the dangers and to check liver function and lipids? This would not be endorsing his action any more than a needle exchange encourages intravenous drug abuse. He may also benefit from the needle exchange. Is it a damage limitation exercise that can be justified?

Getting drugs out of sport

There is a constant battle between those seeking new techniques to detect illicit use of performance-enhancing substances and those who wish to circumvent the rules. Testing is vigorous and can be unannounced and the penalties for being discovered are severe. Nevertheless there are, and always will be, those who attempt to use illicit ways of enhancing performance to get the necessary slight edge that is required to win. From time to time illegal substances are discovered. In British sport this should not be seen as evidence of widespread abuse of drugs but evidence that a vigorous and effective system of monitoring is in place.

Some would argue that the only way to get a 'level playing field' is to lift all bans on drugs and let us push human endurance to the limit. Records have tumbled with new technologies, going back to spikes and starting blocks and including modern running shoes and fibreglass poles for vaulting. Should we encourage the same with pharmacological technology? This is a false argument, as the banned substances are not without significant risk. It cannot even be argued that the athlete is free to make his own choice because if the opposition use drugs to gain advantage, he will have to do the same to be able to compete.

With the upcoming 2012 Olympics in the UK, there is a call to toughen the UK's stance on doping in sport. Various suggestions have been made including the possibility of trialling a doping passport to be carried by all athletes. This would record the results of doping tests and natural concentrations of hormones such as erythropoietin during their careers, the idea being that this would make it easier to detect any substance abuse.

World Anti-Doping Agency

WADA was founded with the belief that 'athletes have a fundamental right to participate in doping-free sport and that doping endangers athlete health and the integrity of sport'. It serves as the independent international body responsible for coordinating and monitoring the global fight against doping in sport.

Last updated: 11 July 2008

⇨ Information from Patient UK. Visit www.patient.co.uk for more.

© EMIS 2010 as distributed at http://www.patient.co.uk/ doctor/Drugs-and-Sport.htm, used with permission

The history of drugs in sport

Information from teachpe.com

The use of drugs in sports with the aim of improving performance is a major problem for sports governing bodies. This, however, is not a new phenomenon.

Drugs have been used to enhance performance since ancient times. Greek and Roman civilisations used mushrooms and herbs to improve their performance. Later, in the 19th century, substances including alcohol, opium and caffeine were used.

The more recent forms of performance-enhancing drugs have roots from World War II, when amphetamines were used by American soldiers to keep them alert and Germans used anabolic steroids to increase their aggressive behaviour. A number of deaths and allegations of drug taking encouraged the International Olympic Committee (IOC) to set up a Medical Commission in 1967 which banned the use of drugs and other performance-enhancing substances. Small-scale testing was introduced at the 1968 Mexico Olympics, followed by a full-scale testing at the next Games in Munich, 1972.

> **Drugs have been used to enhance performance since ancient times. Greek and Roman civilisations used mushrooms and herbs to improve their performance**

In 1975 anabolic steroid use was banned following the development of a test, after which there was a surge of disqualifications through steroid use. In 1983, caffeine and testosterone were added to the prohibited list, followed in 1986 by blood doping and EPO in 1990, despite reliable tests for their detection not being available until 2000.

Following a large number of doping offences being committed in the mid-1990s, and the existence of several conflicting organisations, the World Conference on Doping was held in Switzerland in 1999. As a result, the World Anti-Doping Agency (WADA) was formed to promote and co-ordinate the fight against drug use in sport on an international level, across all sports. WADA was set up under the initiative of the IOC and with the support of other international organisations and governments. The organisation is formed by individuals from the IOC and public authorities.

Why do athletes take drugs?

There are a large number of reasons why an athlete may decide to take drugs. A selection are listed here:

⇨ Pressure to succeed, either from themselves or coaches/family.

⇨ Belief that their competitors are taking drugs.

⇨ Pressure from governments/national authorities (as occurred in the eastern bloc countries in the 1960s and 1970s).

⇨ Financial rewards for outstanding performance.

⇨ Lack of access to, or funding for, training facilities and additional support (nutrition, psychological support).

⇨ Community and media attitudes and expectations of success.

⇨ The above information is reprinted with kind permission from teachpe.com

© teachpe.com

Drugs in sport: the debate

Would allowing the use of enhancement drugs undermine the spirit of sport?

By Henry Troy and Helen Birtwistle

Introduction

Much of the build-up and aftermath to Beijing 2008 focused on drugs and how to keep them out of the Olympics. For a long time the treatment of athletes found to be using drugs has been resolute. In 1988 the sprinter Ben Johnson was stripped of his 100m gold medal after testing positive for drugs. The scale and complexity of the problem was made plain in 2000, when two of East Germany's most senior sports officials were charged with systematically doping over 100 young athletes throughout the 1970s and 80s. More recently the British sprinter Dwain Chambers was banned from athletics for two years after testing positive for the anabolic steroid tetrahydrogestrinone (THG). But condemnation of Chambers and others has not been unanimous. The Professional Footballers' Association (PFA) has voiced growing concern about the intrusiveness of drug tests and a number of commentators have suggested that reactions to drug testing are more to do with moral posturing and political opportunism than sportsmanship. Some have further argued that the use of performance-enhancing drugs is entirely consistent with the desire to reach new heights of human athleticism. But many remain vehemently anti-drugs, claiming that they undermine the spirit of sport. If drugs were allowed, the most successful athletes may not be the fastest or strongest, but those who have the best medical team. So would sport be undermined by sportsmen pumping themselves full of drugs? Or is doping in the tradition of what competitors have always done: pushing the boundaries of human endurance?

> **Is doping in the tradition of what competitors have always done: pushing the boundaries of human endurance?**

Drugs level playing field...
androstendiol
danazol
ethylestrenol
metenolone

The drugs in sport debate in context

What is the 'spirit of sport'?

Opponents of enhancement drugs argue that drug-taking shows bad sportsmanship and deprives athletes of the 'level playing field' so central to the idea of fair competition. Recalling Pierre de Coubertin, the founder of the modern Olympic Games', famous maxim 'The important thing in the Olympic Games is not winning but taking part', some claim that winning at any cost has superseded other considerations and is ultimately undermining the dignity and integrity of sport. But, say others, times have changed. Winning has acquired a stronger emphasis, but this is no bad thing. The shift from amateurism to professionalism in the Olympics, and in sport more widely, has improved the quality of sport and helped produce better athletes. Another definition of the 'spirit of sport' – the Olympian motto 'Citius, Altius, Fortius' (faster, higher, stronger) – implies sport is about exploring and stretching the limits of human potential. Its proponents suggest that the attempt to overcome natural limits is what differentiates human athletic goals from those of animals. The use of enhancement drugs, they argue, is a fundamentally human activity. But others disagree. They argue that drug intervention can reach a point where it is impossible to distinguish between the uniqueness of human achievement and technological innovation. There are innate biological limits that athletes should respect and which give meaning to sporting excellence. Allowing enhancement drugs would de-humanise sport.

Opponents of enhancement drugs argue that drug-taking shows bad sportsmanship and deprives athletes of the 'level playing field' so central to the idea of fair competition

What are performance-enhancing drugs?

The practice of using artificial substances or methods to enhance athletic performance has a long history. As far back as the 776 BC Olympics, athletes were using cola plants and even eating sheep's testicles in an effort to boost performance. Manipulation of the body, whether through training, diet or the use of equipment, was, and continues to be, an accepted part of athletic activity. What, ask critics, is so different about chemical enhancers, or even genetic enhancement? But strict limits are placed on the types of enhancers that can be legitimately used by athletes and there are currently eight main categories of enhancement drugs banned by the World Anti-Doping Agency. Advancements in biotechnologies in the last four decades now mean that athletes can use a cocktail of drugs to overcome physical barriers, including anabolic steroids, Beta 2, blood doping and oxygen carriers. But whilst these drugs remain illegal in competitive sport, developments in performance-enhancing technologies are growing by the day. Not only have researchers in London created a muscle-building DNA, but more recently Henning Wackerhage, a scientist and former triathlon competitor, laid out the possibility of modifying the human genome to create a superhuman runner.

Is doping dangerous?

Anabolic steroids can cause infertility, liver abnormalities and tumours and various psychiatric disorders. Androstenedione will increase your chances of having a heart attack or stroke. Critics of enhancement drugs argue that they pose a significant health risk for athletes. But isn't trying to be the best already hard on your health? Exercise is known to be healthy, but the extreme exercise many athletes put themselves through can also be damaging. But critics say that the dangers posed by enhancement drugs are very different. Evidence given by the young female athletes involved in the German doping scandal revealed that forced steroids and testosterone doping had done profound physical damage, including liver dysfunction and infertility. Those that questioned the procedure were told that 'you eat the pills, or you die!'. The scandal thus also raises important questions about coercion in sport. Attractive as narratives of the 'human will' and 'assertion' are, can the decision to use performance-enhancing drugs ever be a wholly autonomous one?

About Debating Matters

Debating matters because ideas matter. This is the premise of the Institute of Ideas Debating Matters Competition for sixth-form students which emphasises substance over style, and the importance of taking ideas seriously. Debating Matters represents a challenging and engaging format, presenting students with topical debates that will appeal to students from a wide range of backgrounds, and to schools with a long tradition of debating, or with none. The competition takes ideas, argument and young people seriously, encouraging students to engage in an intelligent contest of ideas and holding up their ideas to critical scrutiny.

January 2009

⇨ The above information is reprinted with kind permission from the Institute of Ideas Debating Matters Competition. Visit www.debatingmatters.com for more information.

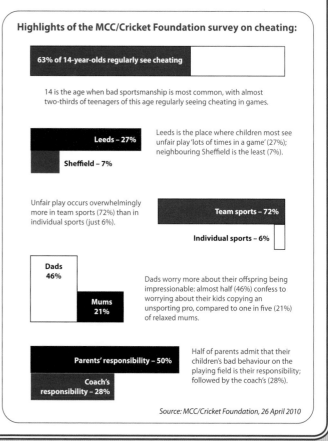

Highlights of the MCC/Cricket Foundation survey on cheating:

63% of 14-year-olds regularly see cheating

14 is the age when bad sportsmanship is most common, with almost two-thirds of teenagers of this age regularly seeing cheating in games.

Leeds – 27%

Sheffield – 7%

Leeds is the place where children most see unfair play 'lots of times in a game' (27%); neighbouring Sheffield is the least (7%).

Unfair play occurs overwhelmingly more in team sports (72%) than in individual sports (just 6%).

Team sports – 72%

Individual sports – 6%

Dads 46%

Mums 21%

Dads worry more about their offspring being impressionable: almost half (46%) confess to worrying about their kids copying an unsporting pro, compared to one in five (21%) of relaxed mums.

Parents' responsibility – 50%

Coach's responsibility – 28%

Half of parents admit that their children's bad behaviour on the playing field is their responsibility; followed by the coach's (28%).

Source: MCC/Cricket Foundation, 26 April 2010

INSTITUTE OF IDEAS DEBATING MATTERS COMPETITION

Performance-enhancing drugs should be allowed in sport

Opening and closing statements from the Oxford debate on this motion, which took place in June 2010.

Proposer's opening statement – by Julian Savulescu

Two great sporting events are about to commence: Le Tour de France and the Football World Cup. Doping will play a part in both of these. In every professional sport where doping could confer an advantage, there is doping. Even if it is not widespread and even if you don't know about it.

This is most obvious in Le Tour. Since it began in 1903, riders have used drugs to cope with the ordeal, resorting to alcohol, caffeine, cocaine, amphetamines, steroids, growth hormone, erythropoietin (EPO) and blood doping. But all sports, even the World Cup, face the drug problem. The enormous rewards for the winner, the effectiveness of the drugs and the low rate of testing all create a cheating 'game' that has proved irresistible to some athletes. It is irresistible because of human nature. And the cheating athletes are now winning.

> **A rational, realistic approach to doping would be to allow safe performance-enhancing drugs which are consistent with the spirit of a particular sport, and to focus on evaluating athletes' health**

Drugs such as EPO and growth hormone are natural chemicals in the body and are hard to detect. And the task will get tougher still. Athletes have returned to simple blood doping (having their own blood donated prior to competition and retransfused during the event), which is virtually impossible to detect if done properly. Gene doping, for example, will be equally difficult to detect. This is a technique which allows the introduction of genes into an athlete's own genetic material, or DNA, to improve muscular strength or endurance.

Also, the injection of an insulin-like growth factor (proven to increase muscle strength in mice) into the muscles of athletes would be simple. Detection would require muscle biopsy, slicing a core of muscle to examine under a microscope, which would be dangerous and difficult. EPO genes could also be directly integrated into athletes' DNA. Such gene therapy already works in monkeys.

There are only two options. We can try to ratchet up the war on doping. But this will fail, as the war on all victimless crimes involving personal advantage have failed (look at the war on alcohol, drugs and prostitution). Or we can regulate the use of performance-enhancing drugs.

Some performance enhancers which were once illegal, such as caffeine, have been legalised because they are safe enough. This has had no adverse effects on sport and has removed the necessity of policing a ban and the problem of cheating.

Some controversy could have been avoided if we allowed riders to take EPO or blood dope up to some safe level, for example where their red blood cells make up 50 per cent of their blood. This level is deemed safe by the International Cycling Union and this level is easily detected by a simple, reliable and cheap blood test. Other drugs such as growth hormone can be monitored by evaluating athletes' health, looking for signs of excess, rather than trying to detect what is a normal hormone.

A rational, realistic approach to doping would be to allow safe performance-enhancing drugs which are consistent with the spirit of a particular sport, and to focus on evaluating athletes' health. Some interventions would change the nature of a sport, like creating webbed hands

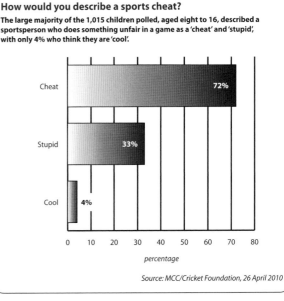

How would you describe a sports cheat?
The large majority of the 1,015 children polled, aged eight to 16, described a sportsperson who does something unfair in a game as a 'cheat' and 'stupid', with only 4% who think they are 'cool'.

percentage

Source: MCC/Cricket Foundation, 26 April 2010

Category	Percentage
Cheat	72%
Stupid	33%
Cool	4%

UNIVERSITY OF OXFORD

and feet in swimming, and should be banned on those grounds. But the use of drugs to increase endurance is a part of sport's history.

The rules of a sport are not God-given, but are primarily there for four reasons. They:

1 define the nature of a particular display of physical excellence;

2 create conditions for fair competition;

3 protect health;

4 provide a spectacle.

Any rule must be enforceable. The current zero tolerance of drugs fails on the last three grounds and is unenforceable. The rules can be changed. We can better protect the health of competitors by allowing access to safe performance-enhancement and monitoring their health. We provide a better spectacle if we give up the futile search for undetectable drugs, and focus on measurable issues relevant to the athlete's health.

Given the pay-offs in terms of glory and money, some athletes will always access a black market of dangerous banned drugs which confer an extra advantage. But overall, regulated access is better than prohibition, as the honest athletes presently have no access to performance-enhancers.

Under a regulated market, they would have access to some safe performance-enhancers. This would narrow the advantage gap between the cheats and the honest athletes. And we would create a stimulus for the market to produce new, safe performance-enhancers. Limited resources could be better deployed to detect the dangerous drugs.

The World Anti-Doping Agency (WADA) claims that performance enhancement is against the spirit of sport. But caffeine does not appear to have corrupted the Olympics. Athletes already radically change their bodies through advanced, technologically-driven training regimes. Tour riders receive intravenous artificial nutrition and hydration overnight because their bodies cannot take on enough food and fluid naturally.

Ben Johnson, stripped of his 100m Olympic gold at the 1988 Games, said that the human body was not designed to run the speeds it is called upon to run now, and steroids were necessary to recover from the gruelling training and injuries. Jacques Anquetil, the great French cyclist, once asked a French politician if 'they expect us to ride the Tour on mineral water'. Far from demonising these great athletes, we should admire them.

The use of drugs to accelerate recovery and to enhance the expression of human ability are a part of the spirit of sport. Some drugs, such as the modest use of EPO or growth hormone, can enhance the expression of physical excellence in sport. The challenge is to understand the spirit of each sport, and which drugs are consistent with this. But performance enhancement *per se* is not against the spirit of sport; it is the spirit of sport. To choose to be better is to be human.

What is ruining sport is cheating. But cheating can be reduced by changing the rules. Cheating can be better reduced by allowing drugs rather than banning them.

Opposer's opening statement – by John William Devine

In just over two years the world's elite athletes will descend on the UK for London 2012. Should these athletes be permitted to use performance-enhancing drugs or should the fight to eliminate such drugs from sport continue? The World Anti-Doping Agency (WADA) maintains that the use of performance-enhancing drugs (doping) is contrary to the 'spirit of sport'. While WADA's account of the spirit of sport is frustratingly underdeveloped, the idea that the purpose of sport provides reason to prohibit doping captures something important.

Rules in sport are designed in part so that success can be achieved only by competitors who display certain excellences of body, mind and will. Practices which impair the display of these excellences should be prohibited. The use of a stepladder in the high jump, a catapult in the javelin, or a bicycle in the marathon, all prevent the relevant excellences (jumping, throwing and running) being displayed. To call any of these practices an 'enhancement' in these events is a misnomer. Far from improving performance, their use obscures the display of the relevant excellences. Such practices undermine the integrity of these sports and, consequently, are rightly prohibited.

Doping is similarly liable to undermine the integrity of sport. It can do this either by preventing a relevant excellence from being displayed at all, or by elevating one type of excellence to an unwarranted level of importance.

To demonstrate the first threat to the integrity of sport posed by doping, consider the case of archery. Part of the challenge of archery is to maintain near-perfect balance so that one's shot is not misdirected by, among other things, an unsteady or nervous hand. The use of beta-blockers to reduce one's natural tremor is rightly prohibited in archery and other target sports like shooting. By reducing the natural tremor, beta-blockers serve to remove one of the excellences that the sport is designed to call forth in competitors. While beta-blockers may increase the accuracy of a competitor's shots, the sport is the worse for their use because the user's performance displays a narrower range of excellences.

Next, consider high-risk sports like rugby, boxing, or American football. One of the excellences that outstanding athletes in these sports display is the control of fear. If rugby players doped in a way that dampened their fear of physical injury then their performance would in a certain respect be less admirable. Such a drug would prevent the player from displaying the courage that is partly constitutive of the excellence of a rugby player.

As the above examples suggest, supposed enhancements can undermine the integrity of a sport by hindering or preventing the display of excellences around which the sport is organised. However, not only are the rules of sport organised around the display of different types of excellence, they are organised so that different excellences contribute to performance to different degrees.

Rules in sport are designed in part so that success can be achieved only by competitors who display certain excellences of body, mind and will

Andy Murray will lead British hopes at this month's Wimbledon Championships with a playing style based on patience, deftness of touch and strategic nous. It was precisely these excellences that were threatened in the Championships of the 1990s. As players grew stronger and racquets became more powerful, power servers became dominant. One type of excellence – powerful serving – assumed too much prominence in the style of tennis that prevailed at the time. Players with games based around the display of excellences like Murray's found it increasingly difficult to succeed.

In response to this trend, adjustments were made to the court surface and ball pressure to encourage longer, more strategic rallies. These efforts to slow down the game might be best explained as an attempt to redress the 'balance of excellences' in the sport: that is, to reshape the playing conditions so that a broader range of excellences valued in the sport could be displayed in the performance of those successful in the sport.

Doping poses a similar threat to the balance of excellence in different sports. Lifting the ban on doping would unduly elevate in importance the capacity to metabolise performance-enhancing substances. In addition, the effects of their use on the performance of athletes may elevate certain excellences like power and speed at the expense of others, in a similar way to that which occurred in Wimbledon. Thus, the importance of other excellences in performance would be diminished in a way that is inconsistent with the purposes around which the sport is organised.

We began by endorsing WADA's 'spirit of sport' justification for the ban on doping but we have reason to disagree with their positing a single list of banned substances to apply across all sports (with individual sports having only the option to add to the list for their purposes). Different sports are organised around different excellences. Consequently, different types of drugs will threaten the integrity of different sports in different ways. We should tailor doping policy to individual sports or at least to clusters of sports. Sporting authorities, in consultation with players, coaches and fans need to reflect on what excellences should be prized in their respective sports. This background understanding of the purpose of the sport provides the necessary context within which a debate about doping can take place.

What is at stake in this debate is not just the health of our athletes or the fairness of competition but the very purpose of sport. We must fiercely oppose the pernicious effects of doping so we can ensure that what we celebrate in London 2012 are not tainted performances but rather outstanding displays of authentic sporting excellence. *June 2010*

⇨ This article is an extract from the Oxford online debate 'Performance enhancing drugs should be allowed in sport', which was first published on the University of Oxford website (www.ox.ac.uk) in June 2010 and also the Oxford Uehiro Centre for Practical Ethics website (www.practicalethics.ox.ac.uk) and blog (www. practicalethicsnews.com).

THAT'S NOT SPORT...

UNIVERSITY OF OXFORD

Sport cheats are bottom of the class in pupil poll

Information from Chance to Shine.

As part of the re-launch of MCC Spirit of Cricket in Chance to Shine schools from today (26 April), the Cricket Foundation and MCC have commissioned a survey on poor sportsmanship, from grassroots to the elite end of sport.

The research finds that professional sportsmen who break the rules are not 'cool for school', and young fans are not as impressionable as we might think.

Three-quarters of the 1,015 children aged eight to 16 polled describe a sportsperson who does something unfair in a game as a 'cheat' (72%) and 'stupid' (33%), with only 4% describing them as 'cool'.

Far from being easily influenced, two-thirds of children (67%) deny that seeing a famous sportsperson doing something unfair in order to win would make them more likely to do it themselves.

However, the school playing field is still a hotbed of rule breaking with more than half of children (54%) witnessing unfair play in every single game they play. Faking injuries, elbowing in the face, arguing with the umpire and head butting are among the many examples of gamesmanship that youngsters give in the poll.

Encouragingly, in a like-for-like survey of 200 eight- to 11-year-olds involved in the MCC Spirit of Cricket scheme, the number of children who witness unfair play in every game drops significantly to 37%. Equally, the number of children who say they 'hardly ever' or 'never' see unfair play (41%) is twice that of children who are not part of the fair play scheme (21%).

Other highlights of the MCC/Cricket Foundation national survey include:

⇨ 14 is the age when bad sportsmanship is most common, with almost two-thirds (63%) of teenagers of this age regularly seeing cheating in games.

⇨ Leeds is the place where children most see unfair play 'lots of times in a game' (27%), neighbouring Sheffield is the least (7%).

⇨ Unfair play occurs overwhelmingly more in team sports (72%) than in individual sports (just 6%).

⇨ Dads worry more about their offspring being impressionable: almost half (46%) confess to worrying about their kids copying an unsporting pro, compared to one in five (21%) of relaxed mums.

⇨ Half of parents admit that their children's bad behaviour on the playing field is their responsibility; followed by the coach's (28%).

Spirit of sport hall of shame

Former boxing champion Mike Tyson's notorious bite on Evander Holyfield's ear in their 1997 heavyweight title match is voted the worst act of bad sportsmanship. Tyson receives a quarter (26%) of parents' votes.

Thierry Henry's double handball against the Republic of Ireland in last year's World Cup qualifier earns him second spot in the 'Spirit of Sport Hall of Shame', surprisingly ahead of Diego Maradona's infamous 'Hand of God' act, which is ranked third.

26 April 2010

⇨ The above information is reprinted with kind permission from the Cricket Foundation's Chance to Shine campaign. Visit www.chancetoshine.org for more.

© *The Cricket Foundation's Chance to Shine campaign*

British athletes face up to £1,000 fine for missing drug tests

Athletes in Britain will be fined up to £1,000 for missing drug tests or failing to update details of their whereabouts as part of tough new anti-doping measures announced on Thursday.

By Simon Hart

The fines, which will be increased for a second missed test, are aimed at avoiding a repeat of the Christine Ohuruogu saga in 2006 when the Olympic 400m champion was banned for a year for missing three random drug tests.

Since then the number of missed tests has declined sharply and there are currently no British athletes with two missed tests against their name, but the new financial penalties will be written into athletes' contracts in April to reinforce the message about being available for testing.

The changes were announced on Thursday by the former Paralympian, Dame Tanni Grey-Thompson, who was commissioned by UK Athletics to chair an independent review of the governing body's anti-doping rules. Ohuruogu was one of numerous British athletes she consulted.

'Education is very important but you also need something for the athletes to understand,' said Grey-Thompson. 'I think the athletes have been through a massive learning curve in the last couple of years in terms of understanding what whereabouts is all about and for me it's a central part of being an elite athlete.'

She added: 'It's about the carrot and the stick because people react to different things. Some people react better to a carrot and some people react better to a stick.'

The fines are one of 22 recommendations made by Grey-Thompson, all of which have been adopted by the UK Athletics board. She was joined on the review panel by former athletes Colin Jackson and Ed Moses, PR expert Mike Lee and the former head of anti-doping at UK Sport, John Scott.

Their recommendations include a new rule designed to avoid a repetition of last year's controversy over Dwain Chambers, whom the governing body tried unsuccessfully to ban on the grounds that he had not been available for drug testing before his return to athletics.

From now on, anyone who has not been subject to continuous out-of-competition testing will have to serve a one-year 'quarantine period' before they are eligible to compete for Britain.

The rule is not retrospective and does not affect Chambers' plans to qualify for this year's European Indoors in Turin and the World Championships in Berlin.

Athletes who are ineligible for a championship will also be barred from competing at the UK trials for that event, even if they double up as the national championships. Last year, Chambers won the 100m at the Olympic trials in Birmingham, despite being banned from the Olympics.

One novel idea being adopted by UK Athletics is the introduction of drug tests for all employees, including office staff.

Niels de Vos, the UK Athletics' chief executive, said: 'It's about making sure that everybody in the organisation understands and lives by the same rules.'

22 January 2009

THE TELEGRAPH

⇨ In a Government survey, during the week prior to the interview just over one in five 5- to 19-year-olds (21%) had taken part in three hours or more organised sport. 47% had done no organised sport. (page 1)

⇨ Boys are significantly more likely than girls to have participated in three or more hours (26% vs. 16%). Girls are more likely than boys to have been completely inactive (52% vs. 43%). (page 1)

⇨ A change to distribution of Lottery money will see £50m more come to sport annually from 2012. (page 6)

⇨ A survey has shown that people in Britain think that a fair average salary for a professional footballer would be £62,000 per year. Premiership players all earn between £1 million and £5 million per year. (page 11)

⇨ Some football clubs are paying 85% of their income out in players' wages. The result is that in the end they make losses and are effectively bankrupt. (page 12)

⇨ The latest statistics revealed during the 2008/09 football season: 3,752 arrests were made at domestic and international matches in England and Wales. (page 13)

⇨ London 2012 will make history as the first Games to have representation by men and women in every sport. (page 19)

⇨ There have been a number of cases in which women athletes have been 'accused' of being men masquerading as women to gain advantage over other women competitors; there is no similar history in the Olympics of women being 'accused' of masquerading as men. (page 19)

⇨ There are a wide range of sports that people in wheelchairs can play. These include sports such as archery, athletics (track and field), wheelchair basketball, bowls, cue sports (snooker and nine-ball pool), wheelchair rugby, wheelchair racing (road), fencing, handcycling, powerlifting, racquetball, swimming, table tennis and tennis. (page 20)

⇨ Sport is divided into classifications: for example, men compete separately to women; in combat sports people compete by body weight. In disabled sport, classification is the method by which fair and equitable competition is achieved. (page 21)

⇨ There are only seven British Asian players in professional football and a Commission for Racial Equality (CRE) survey into professional football in 2004 revealed that in total there were only ten Asian players at Premier League club academies. (page 24)

⇨ Football is Britain's national game. Yet in 2009 not one gay professional footballer in Britain, of which there are undoubtedly many, feels that football is an industry in which it is safe to be openly gay. (page 26)

⇨ An athlete can be called for drug testing at any time, in or out of competition. During competition, some sports only carry out drug testing on the winning team or top three competitors. Others will test by random selection from all competitors. (page 27)

⇨ The problem of stimulants in sport reached public attention in 1960 when the Danish cyclist Knut Jenson died in the Rome Olympics and it transpired that he had been taking amphetamines. (page 29)

⇨ The World Anti-Doping Agency (WADA) serves as the independent international body responsible for coordinating and monitoring the global fight against doping in sport. (page 31)

⇨ As far back as the 776 BC Olympics, athletes were using cola plants and even eating sheep's testicles in an effort to boost performance. (page 34)

⇨ 14 is the age when bad sportsmanship is most common, with almost two-thirds (63%) of teenagers of this age regularly seeing cheating in games. (page 38)

⇨ Unfair play occurs overwhelmingly more in team sports (72%) than in individual sports (just 6%). (page 38)

Anabolic steroids

'Anabolic steroid' is a blanket term for drugs which mimic the effects of male reproductive hormones, i.e. by boosting muscle growth and protein synthesis. Side effects such as aggression, liver damage and high blood pressure can be very harmful. Some athletes take them illegally in order to improve their performance.

Athlete

A highly-trained professional or amateur sportsperson.

Diuretics

A chemical that can be ingested by athletes, increasing the excretion of water from their body during urination. This is done in order to hide banned substances during urine tests, as urine is more diluted. Diuretic use in sporting competitions is illegal.

Doping

The use of performance-enhancing drugs by athletes during sporting competitions. Most of these drugs are illegal and players are required by law to take a drugs test before taking part in competitive events. If it is found that they have taken drugs they will automatically be disqualified from the event, and may also be banned from taking part in any future competitions for a specified period of time.

Hooliganism

A popular term in the past for violence at football matches. Match organisers have worked very hard in recent years to combat hooliganism. Police and other security measures are now routinely put in place to control rioting fans, and repeat 'football hooligans' can be banned from travelling abroad to attend games.

Inclusive sport

Sport which is inclusive does not discriminate on the grounds of gender, ethnicity, sexual orientation or disability. Sport is usually segregated where athletes have a physical difference which makes equal competition difficult – men and women do not generally compete against each other, for example, nor disabled and able-bodied athletes. This is called classification. However, there is no ban on any athlete competing in a separate competition. This is why the term 'sport equity' is sometimes used rather than equality. Athletes should be protected from discrimination and unfair treatment, such as racist and homophobic chanting at football matches.

London 2012

Every four years the Olympic Games are held in a different city around the world. The next summer Olympic Games, which will take place in 2012, are to be held in London, Great Britain.

Paralympic Games

The Paralympic Games are a series of sporting competitions open to athletes with physical disabilities. They are held immediately following the Olympic Games. Athletes with disabilities including amputations, paralysis and blindness take part in a wide range of competitive sports. The next summer Paralympics will be held in London in 2012.

Stimulants

A drug which causes a temporary improvement in mental or physical functioning.

Wage cap

There is often controversy over the salaries paid to some football players. The highest-paid player in 2010 was Real Madrid's Cristiano Ronaldo, who earned £11.3 million. Some people consider such large sums to be unfair and disproportionate, and in many cases they can nearly bankrupt a club. A wage cap would prevent a player from earning over a specified amount, or a set percentage of the football club's profits. However, critics argue that if this were imposed in the UK, many of the best football players would move to clubs overseas.

WAGs

The abbreviation WAG stands for 'Wives And Girlfriends', and has become a popular label for the partners of footballers. The WAGs are associated with designer clothes and glamorous lifestyles and receive a lot of attention from the media.

Additional Resources

Other Issues titles

If you are interested in researching further some of the issues raised in *Sport and Society,* you may like to read the following titles in the *Issues* series:

⇨ Vol. 197 *Living with Disability* (ISBN 978 1 86168 557 5)

⇨ Vol. 194 *Responsible Drinking* (ISBN 978 1 86168 555 1)

⇨ Vol. 188 *Tobacco and Health* (ISBN 978 1 86168 539 1)

⇨ Vol. 186 *Cannabis Use* (ISBN 978 1 86168 527 8)

⇨ Vol. 184 *Understanding Eating Disorders* (ISBN 978 1 86168 525 4)

⇨ Vol. 176 *Health Issues for Young People* (ISBN 978 1 86168 500 1)

⇨ Vol. 172 *Racial and Ethnic Discrimination* (ISBN 978 1 86168 486 8)

⇨ Vol. 170 *Body Image and Self-Esteem* (ISBN 978 1 86168 484 4)

⇨ Vol. 163 *Drugs in the UK* (ISBN 978 1 86168 456 1)

⇨ Vol. 162 *Staying Fit* (ISBN 978 1 86168 455 4)

⇨ Vol. 154 *The Gender Gap* (ISBN 978 1 86168 441 7)

⇨ Vol. 153 *Sexual Orientation and Society* (ISBN 978 1 86168 440 0)

⇨ Vol. 142 *Media Issues* (ISBN 978 1 86168 408 0)

⇨ Vol. 134 *Customers and Consumerism* (ISBN 978 1 86168 386 1)

For a complete list of available *Issues* titles, please visit our website: www.independence.co.uk/shop

Useful organisations

You may find the websites of the following organisations useful for further research:

⇨ **Chance to Shine:** www.chancetoshine.org

⇨ **Department for Children, Schools and Families:** www.dcsf.gov.uk

⇨ **Department for Culture, Media and Sport:** www.culture.gov.uk

⇨ **The Football League:** www.football-league.co.uk

⇨ **Institute of Ideas Debating Matters:** www.debatingmatters.com

⇨ **Kick It Out:** www.kickitout.org

⇨ **LSIS Excellence Gateway:** www.excellencegateway.org.uk

⇨ **Patient UK:** www.patient.co.uk

⇨ **Sport England:** www.sportengland.org

⇨ **Stonewall:** www.stonewall.org.uk

⇨ **teachpe:** www.teachpe.com

⇨ **TheSite:** www.thesite.org

⇨ **UK Sport:** www.uksport.gov.uk

⇨ **University of Manchester:** www.manchester.ac.uk

⇨ **University of Oxford:** www.ox.ac.uk

⇨ **WheelPower:** www.wheelpower.org.uk

For more book information, visit our website...

www.independence.co.uk

Information available online includes:

✓ Detailed descriptions of titles

✓ Tables of contents

✓ Facts and figures

✓ Online ordering facilities

✓ Log-in page for Issues Online (an Internet resource available free to Firm Order Issues subscribers – ask your librarian to find out if this service is available to you)

ACKNOWLEDGEMENTS

The publisher is grateful for permission to reproduce the following material.

While every care has been taken to trace and acknowledge copyright, the publisher tenders its apology for any accidental infringement or where copyright has proved untraceable. The publisher would be pleased to come to a suitable arrangement in any such case with the rightful owner.

Chapter One: Sporting Trends

Children and young people's participation in organised sport, © Ipsos MORI, *School cricket scheme teaches pupils 'the three Fs': Fitness, Friendship and Fair play,* © The Cricket Foundation's Chance to Shine campaign, *Pupils' sporting participation [graphs],* © Crown copyright is reproduced with the permission of Her Majesty's Stationery Office, *Olympic-style sports competition for young people launched as part of 2012 legacy,* © Crown copyright is reproduced with the permission of Her Majesty's Stationery Office, *David Cameron's sport cuts will leave Britain playing catch-up for years,* © Guardian News and Media Limited 2010, *Time spent participating in organised sport outside of the school day [graph],* © Ipsos MORI, *How to build the perfect athlete,* © Guardian News and Media Limited 2010, *Sports and activities provided during the 2008/09 academic year [graph],* © Crown copyright is reproduced with the permission of Her Majesty's Stationery Office, *The politics of football: should footballers be wage capped?,* © LSIS Excellence Gateway, *Violence down at football grounds,* © The Football League, *Sports stars are no role models, say scientists,* © University of Manchester, *Why do women want to be WAGs?,* © Guardian News and Media Limited 2010, *Proportion of men and women who take part in sport by age [graph],* © Women's Sport and Fitness Foundation.

Chapter Two: Inclusion in Sport

Investing in inclusive sport, © Sport England, *2012 to make history as first gender equality Games,* © Sport England, *Sport, sex and gender,* © The British Library Board, *Wheelchair sport FAQs,* © WheelPower 2010, *Talent initiative gives Britain's Paralympic potential a boost,* © UK Sport 2010, *Exercising with health problems,* © TheSite.org, *Trends for top 15 female participation sports [graph],* © Women's Sport and Fitness Foundation, *Asians in football,* © Kick It Out, *Proportion of women and men who take part in sport by gender and ethnicity,* © Women's Sport and Fitness Foundation, *Homophobia in football,* © Kick It Out, *Leagues behind: football's failure to tackle anti-gay abuse,* © Stonewall.

Chapter Three: Doping

Types of drug testing in sport, © teachpe.com, *Drugs and sport,* © EMIS 2010 as distributed at http://www.patient.co.uk/doctor/Drugs-and-Sport.htm, used with permission, *The history of drugs in sport,* © teachpe.com, *Drugs in sport: the debate,* © Institute of Ideas Debating Matters Competition, *Highlights of the MCC/Cricket Foundation survey on cheating [graphs],* © MCC/Cricket Foundation, *Performance-enhancing drugs should be allowed in sport,* © University of Oxford, *How would you describe a sports cheat? [graph],* © MCC/Cricket Foundation, *Sports cheats are bottom of the class in pupil poll,* © The Cricket Foundation's Chance to Shine campaign, *British athletes face up to £1,000 fine for missing drug tests,* © Telegraph Media Group Limited 2010.

Illustrations

Pages 1, 14, 30, 37: Simon Kneebone; pages 3, 25, 32, 38: Don Hatcher; pages 10, 31: Bev Aisbett; pages 13, 27, 33, 39: Angelo Madrid.

Cover photography

Left: © Einar Hansen. Centre: © Gabriella Fabbri. Right: © Pierre Benker.

Additional acknowledgements

Research by Lauren Hart. Additional research and editorial by Carolyn Kirby on behalf of Independence.

And with thanks to the Independence team: Mary Chapman, Sandra Dennis and Jan Sunderland.

Lisa Firth
Cambridge
September, 2010